The Crosses I've Carried

MELANIE CLARK

Fulton Books
Meadville, PA

Published by Fulton Books 2025

ISBN 979-8-89427-267-2 (paperback)
ISBN 979-8-89427-268-9 (digital)

Printed in the United States of America

I remember my mother always saying God doesn't give crosses to those who cannot carry them.

Thank you. These words always gave me strength to fight and move forward.

People may question if a hard life is truly God's will. It may be.

I want to thank every beautiful soul that has touched my life.

Contents

My Dream

I run for the door of the basement, "Deshawn, it's the police— a drug raid. Get rid of the stuff!" I yell as I run down the steps. There is a look of madness and panic in Deshawn's eyes; he is scared.

Deshawn reaches into his pocket and pulls out a handful of crack in baggies. It is so loud upstairs— police yelling, things being thrown around, crashing sounds, footsteps thumping, sirens, all mixed with my heart pounding in my chest. All I can think is, *This can't be happening again, and this time, Deshawn has drugs on him. He's going to get caught!* Deshawn takes a quick glance at me, his eyes feverish and beads of sweat covering his face. Then suddenly, impulsively, he throws the whole handful of drugs into his mouth and swallows.

He begins choking; he can't breathe. I scream in panic, "Someone help me please! He can't breathe!" Lifting my eyes slightly, I see a pair of black shoes. As I raise my eyes further, I see the police in their black uniforms, plastic masks covering their faces and shields in their hands. At this moment, I realize that I am screaming, pleading for them to help; I watch helplessly as my man struggles for air, convulsing in deep spasms and gasping to breathe. He reaches out for someone to help. I can't do anything, only cry, as I watch his agony from a distance. I am frozen, transfixed by what is happening.

Yet my eyes are open, my heart races, and my body is drenched in sweat… Slowly, my mind begins to focus, and shadows merge into solid forms; it is just a dream. Tentatively, I extend my hand; Deshawn is lying beside me, sound asleep. I roll toward him and snuggle up close, placing my hand on his chest to make sure that he is still breathing. My head rises and falls gently, assuming the rhythm of his breathing; everything is okay. Still, I am troubled; why did I have this dream? What does this dream signify? Was it a portent of the future? In retrospect, yes. Ironically, just a mere two months later, real life would prove to be worse than this nightmare, and there would be no waking reprieve. My life would rapidly take a drastic turn. I can still remember that awful day. I relive it over and over in my memory each night when I extend my hand and find the pillow next to me empty. There is no substance, only dreams. But now the dream has become reality, and reality, the way I want things to be, has become the stuff of dreams.

Because of Trust

"They had a forbidden love like Romeo and Juliet, and it ended just as tragically."

It seems as though we were together just the other day, but it's been years now since I last saw his smile, heard his laugh, and most importantly of all, since he last told me "I love you."

I cling to these words; they have become an external expression, representative of happier times.

During these past several years, there remain a lot of unanswered questions and a plethora of haunting images surrounding the death of my boyfriend. On March 16, 1995, my life changed so dramatically; it is a date forever etched in my mind. A part of me died that day along with him.

How could I have been so blind? Did I refuse to admit to myself that he was in trouble? Did I not want to admit stormy clouds into my relationship? Why did I ignore the signs? Why didn't I intervene more strongly? Why, why, why?

I had just started a new job at Walmart and was attending training sessions. The first session was just about to finish when my trainer received word that I had someone waiting for me up front at the service desk.

Sitting at a table with four other new employees, I just rested my elbow on the table and placed my chin on the palm of my upturned hand and smiled. I shook my head, thinking, *It must be Deshawn, He probably wants the car for something, or maybe he just misses me.* My boss told me to go up to the service desk and see what was up, handing me a copy of my schedule as I left. I felt so confident at this moment, happy I guess that I got the job.

Suddenly, the receiving doors flew open. My friend Andie, my boyfriend's cousin Latoya, and a good friend of his named Tay Tay ran through the receiving doors, running toward me with blank expressions on their faces and tears pouring from their eyes.

Trembling with a feeling of fear and dread in my heart, I managed to blurt out, "What's wrong?"

"It's Deshawn," Andie managed to say between sobs. "He's been shot!" She swallowed hard, looking into my eyes before blurting out again, "He's been shot."

"What?" I screamed in complete shock as I grabbed my heart and shook my head continuously. I was thinking in my mind, *I've got to leave now. He'll be okay. It can't be that bad. He just needs me to be with him.*

But before I could fully contemplate their words or focus my thinking, she said, "He's dead. He's dead, Melanie." Andie just kept repeating these words over and over between gasping sobs.

I immediately lost control and fell to the ground on my knees, burying my face in my hands, crying and screaming "No" out loud.

The next thing I remember were hands attempting to raise me up off the floor, but I couldn't move; I couldn't think. I was paralyzed; all I could do was scream out of agony. The pain was back, and suddenly sharply focused, I cried. I felt as though each sob shattered a part of my soul. There would be little pieces that could never fit together again.

When I finally pulled myself off of the floor, my Walmart trainer had had the room cleared out. She instructed my friends to take me to the chair, but as soon as I sat down, I immediately sprang back up again, overwhelmed with an all-consuming anger. "These people are crazy. I don't want to sit down. I need to go see my man. I want to be with Deshawn right now!"

The drive to the hospital is now nothing more than a vague experience; I was dazed and numb. I didn't know what to do or how to feel. My heart told me to let go, to block it all out…to wall myself up inside.

Finally, I managed to regain my composure enough to ask the others in the car, "How did this happen?"

Tay-Tay turned around, looking at me in the backseat, his voice faltering a little as he tried to speak… Finally, he took a deep breath and replied, "We were in the basement of Deshawn's mother's house, and everyone was playing a game called Trust. It's a game kind of like Russian roulette, but the object of the game is to see if you trust your friend enough that there is not a bullet in the gun, then you pull the trigger."

Crying and upset, I replied, "A game? Playing with a real gun is a game?" Questioning him, I asked, "How come there was a bullet in the gun, if you just said you trust your friend there's not a bullet in the gun?"

"We don't know how the bullet got in the gun" was all he could manage by way of reply.

Feeling disappointed with the answers I'd been given, I felt alone and betrayed. If he was there, he sure acted like he knew very little. My thoughts focused on the question, How could he not know where the bullet came from?

A moment went by; I could feel the pressure of my blood flowing faster and my stomach cramping as I continued to cry. My hand over my mouth started shaking as I mumbled, "Who was in the basement playing this game?"

Tay-Tay spoke with a soft voice, "Deshawn, his brother, David, Deshawn's best friend, Orkey, and a guy named Sawyer and himself."

"Who shot him?" I demanded to know.

"Orkey," he answered with his eyes fixed downward to the floor of the car.

"No," I answered, chewing on my lip, trying to fight this overwhelming rush of sadness.

Tay-Tay just started explaining. "Deshawn had his back turned toward us, and when he turned around, he proceeded to look at Orkey and asked him, 'Do you *trust* that there is not a bullet in this gun? If you do, you will pull the trigger."

It hurt so bad to hear that Orkey shot him, but it hurt me worse that Deshawn acted in this manner of irresponsibility. Deshawn knew I hated guns. "How could he do this to me?" I couldn't even begin to relate how he could chance his own life. "Would he? I don't know."

Crying steadily, I had to know "whose gun were they playing with?"

He said, "I'm not sure. Some say it was David's, and I've heard it could have been Deshawn's."

Well, I have not known Deshawn to have a gun, and I have never seen him with one. If it were David's, who would have a bullet for David's gun but the owner? I thought to myself with an uneasy feeling.

All I could feel at that moment was intense and unbridled anger. I didn't know how to react or who to blame. I sat frozen and alone with my thoughts. I started thinking about last night. David just showed up at our apartment to talk to Deshawn. He wanted Deshawn to hold his gun for him. I was scared; I hated guns. Deshawn never took the gun that night; however, the situation did cause an argument between us. What was his brother doing with a gun and bringing it into our apartment? I was not happy.

I was deeply indulged in my thoughts, then as a sort of afterthought, Tay-Tay added, "Man, I can't believe his tongue fell out of his mouth."

A collective "shh, shh" issued from the others in the car. But it was too late. He hadn't fully considered the consequence of what he had said until after it was said.

I immediately lost control, disturbed by the explicit detail I had just heard. Sobbing uncontrollably, all I could say was "Oh god, help me" as I repeated "His tongue fell out of his mouth. His tongue fell out." Creating an image of the scene and playing everything out in my mind, I was seeing my man's tongue on the floor of the cold, dark, dirty basement floor, reaching out for someone to help, gasping for each breath of air while lying in a pool of blood, while his friends scattered and left him alone after the gun fired. I was worrying if he had been in pain. This was a constant image haunting my instinct. The situations forever intense control over my integrity. "Oh god, how I am hurting inside."

"I wonder if David is still at the police station," Tay-Tay implied to Andie.

I asked curiously, "Why is David at the police station?"

"He took the blame, Melanie, and said he shot Deshawn," Tay-Tay said in a soft tone.

Why would he do that? I thought to myself as we were pulling into the parking lot of the hospital. When Andie shut off the ignition to the car, I was filled with fear. I was too scared to go in. I didn't want to face the actual truth.

The first person I noticed walking into the hospital lobby—crowded with people hollering, screaming, and crying out in pain—was my mother. I was relieved by her presence; I needed her. All I could do was hug her so close to my body as I cried from deep within.

My mother just looked at me, with her eyes swollen and red from the pain she was feeling, saying, "Can you believe this? Why were they playing with guns? How can he be dead, Melanie?"

All I could do was cry and feebly whisper, "I don't know, Mom. I really don't understand anything that has happened."

I was then taken to a small waiting room where his immediate family were mourning over the loss of Deshawn. I can remember the TV as I walked in sluggishly; the announcer was covering the news of Deshawn's fatal accident.

When Katie, Deshawn's mother, saw me, she rose from the seat of her chair and placed her hand gently on my stomach, saying, "This is all we have left of Deshawn, this baby right here." This unborn child was my strength from here on out. My hope to survive.

Still at the hospital, I wanted to see Deshawn. I didn't care what he was going to look like. I just wanted to see him, to feel him next to me. I was not ready to let it all go—to be without his presence, his touch, his voice, his laugh. He was my strength, my hero, my love, my man. I was focused on being by his side.

But Katie and Regina, Deshawn's mother and sister, had already viewed his body. Regina told me that they did not wish for me to view his body at this moment, to wait. "It's not him, Melanie. It just doesn't look like him," Regina said while looking directly into my eyes.

I spoke with a nurse who said if I felt the need to see Deshawn, I was able to, but I had to think about it first. For some reason, I changed my mind. I wanted to remember him the way I last saw him.

Then I started feeling sick; my stomach was aching. I began worrying about my pregnancy. I was thinking to myself, *Is my baby alright?* I began to panic. Everyone around was worried and found a nurse to visit me. The nurse approached me and asked if I felt the need to be examined. I didn't know what to do. I could barely talk; what words I spoke were hard to interpret, for I was crying so hard.

How could this happen? How could this be true? I thought to myself. "Why me?" I asked. I began blaming myself. "If only I was there, this would have never happened."

Finally, my mother and everyone else around had me tell the nurse that I wanted to be looked at. The next thing I knew, I was riding in a wheelchair, with an immense headache. All I could do was bury my face in my hands as people stared at me being wheeled by.

When we entered the room, I was asked to lie on the hospital bed. The nurse proceeded to take my vitals, and they were within normal range. After that, a medical belt was placed around my stomach to monitor the condition of my baby. All I could possibly ask for at this moment was for my unborn child to stay healthy through all this stress brought about during my child's development.

Twenty minutes went by, and I was then released. I was fine, and my baby was too. Hearing my baby's heartbeat gave me a sense of security—that hope to stay strong. I finally calmed down; I really couldn't cry anymore. I just wanted to leave.

I started feeling angry at the doctors and everyone involved. Questions—I had so many. And no one could answer them except for my man, and he was dead. I wanted to know, Did the doctors really try saving his life? Could they have and just didn't or gave up too soon? I was consumed with anger at myself, the world, and with Deshawn. Why did he play that game when he wanted to be a daddy to his child? That's all he talked about. How could he do this to his unborn child and me? But the biggest question no one had an answer to was, How did the bullet get in the gun?

My mother took me over to Deshawn's aunt's house, which was directly across the street from his mother's house, where he was killed. I looked at his mother's house with the yellow tape surrounding the scene of the crime, blocking off anyone from entering, and with police walking around outside and in and out of the house. I realized that I'd never spend another day with him in that house again. How could I attempt to step one foot in that house again? My life just wouldn't be the same. It was so nice out that day, and the sun was shining, as if it were smiling. Everyone was on Conger Street that afternoon.

So many cars were driving by, and people everywhere were talking, crying, and hugging for comfort. I remember one car driving by in particular; to this day, I will never forget. That car's radio was playing "If You're Lonely Now" by K-Ci from the soundtrack of *Jason's Lyric*. I heard that song and thought to myself, *Wait until tonight, girl.*

Deshawn had told me just a few days before that that song reminded him of me. I kept asking him, "Why would this song remind you of me? Are you leaving me?" He never answered, and now, just a few days later, he was gone and I was lonely.

What's really messed up is that the news station and the Waterloo Courier were out on Conger Street talking to family and friends, but not one ever attempted to speak with me. Were they afraid I'd tell them they were wrong? This accident that day was not because of drugs or gangs. It was just young men being stupid or believing that there was nothing wrong with this senseless game they thought was harmless. It's sad to say they had to find out the hard way and lose the life of my man, their friend.

Did they not want to know the true Deshawn and the good man he was? The media these days only focus on the wrong and negative, and if you are black, gangs and drugs must be involved with everything. I was hurt. Why couldn't they focus on what was right and positive? I didn't understand why they wanted to make Deshawn look so bad.

At six o'clock that night, the first thing covered on the news was about the death of Deshawn Price. His picture on the television just tore me up inside. I couldn't take it anymore. I needed to go home.

I don't even remember who took me home that night. I just remember crying myself to sleep and sleeping alone for the first time in months. I remembered smelling the sheets; they smelled of him. I was so alone; Deshawn was not there to hold me and make everything alright. I just lay there, holding my stomach and talking to my child. I just kept repeating, "Mama loves my sweet child, and I'm so sorry this has happened to us."

As I was talking, it made me remember the nights Deshawn and I would lay in bed together and he would place his hand on my stomach. Then the baby would respond and kick. Deshawn would then move his hand to another part of my stomach, and our baby would follow and kick his hand again. We would laugh together. It was like our baby would follow and respond wherever Daddy placed his hand. It was a bond between them—the way they would communicate to one another, "I'm here."

Thinking of that really shook me up. Deshawn would never get to see the moment of our baby's first arrival into this world. He would never get to feel that moment, and we would never get to share that moment together. He would never get to hold our baby. My child would never have the chance to meet Daddy, who was looking forward to meeting his baby. Deshawn was really gone.

I replayed it over and over in my mind. That day, I dropped Deshawn off at his mother's house before I went to Walmart. Deshawn told me that when I would get off work, we would go buy a baby crib. He found one he liked and wanted to buy it and put it up in our apartment that night. I asked him, "Where did you see a baby crib?"

He would not reveal it. "It is a surprise." My eyes were big as my smile grew. We then said "I love you" and kissed each other goodbye.

When he got out of the car and walked across the street, Deshawn turned around, stopped, and just looked at me. He had an inner glow to him that projected. He was just radiantly smiling and looked so happy.

I will never forget that moment because Deshawn never looked back at me like that before; he was really glowing with a bright smile. This was

the last time I saw him alive. It's as if he knew and
was saying goodbye.

Obituary

A precious one from us has gone.
A voice we loved is stilled.
A place is vacant in our home
Which never can be filled.
And after a lonely heartache,
And many a silent tear,
But always a beautiful memory
Of one we loved so dear.

DeShawn Tyrone Price was born to Katie Price and Johnny Sanders on May 9, 1976, in Iowa City at the University of Iowa Hospital.

He attended Waterloo Public Schools. He was an energetic, jolly person and to those who knew him loved him.

He departed this life March 16, 1998 at Allen Hospital.

He leaves to mourn his passing his mother, Katie Price of Waterloo; his father, Johnny Sanders of Iowa City; a step-father, Craig Spencer of Waterloo; two sisters, Louise Brown of Mitchellville and Ragien Bullock of Waterloo; one brother, David Price IV of Waterloo; three step-brothers, six step-sisters, two nieces, Frankie Mae Price and She'Auntore Bullock and a very special companion, Melanie Clark and their expected child and a host of aunts, uncles, cousins and friends.

He was preceded in death by his maternal grandparents, paternal grandparents and a sister, Frannie Mae Price.

Active Pallbearers

David Price IV
Sam Bailey, Jr.
Aster Lewis

Maurice Wilson
Dimitri Harrington
Irvis Williams

Order of Service

Processional

Organist . . . . Mrs. Sherri Phillips
Vocalist . . . . Choir
Scripture . . . . Janet Lewis
Prayer . . . . Minister
Vocalist . . . . Mrs. Sherri Phillips
Poem . . . . Michelle Clark

Acknowledgements and Obituary

Vocalist . . . . Hobart Babe
(Uncle of the deceased)

Eulogy . . . . Pastor Phillips

Renewal and Recessional

●●●●●●●●●●

● Burial ●

Garden of Memories Cemetery
3060 Logan Avenue
Waterloo, Iowa

Chapel Committal Service
Temple of Memories

Gravesite
Garden of the Gleaner Section

Following the graveside service dinner will be served in the church dining hall.

DeShawn
(From the Hebrew root Shawn from John,
an Irish form of John through Sean)

God Is Gracious

— Expression —
is quiet and wise but takes time to be crazy
— Personality —
is very mischievous
— Natural —
he has an artistic ability
— Emotional —
at times, he can be humble
— Character —
is respectful he will be missed
— Physical —
a luminous spirit
— Mental —
has a good imagination and possesses intuitiveness
— Meticulous —
his words are listened to by many.

I Love You, Melanie

Acknowledgements

Perhaps you sent a lovely card,
Or sat quietly in a chair
Perhaps you sent a funeral spray,
If so, we saw it there.
Perhaps you spoke the kindest words,
As any friend could say;
Perhaps you were not there at all,
Just thought of us that day
Whatever you did to console our hearts,
We thank you so much whatever the past.
The family of DeShawn Price

In Loving Memory of

DeShawn Price
the son of Katie Price and Johnny Sanders

Sunrise
Sunday,
May 9th,
1976

Sunset
Thursday,
March 16th,
1998

● Funeral Service ●

Eleven O'clock A.M.
Wednesday, March 22nd, 1998
Christian Fellowship Baptist Church
719 West 6th Street
Waterloo, Iowa
Rev. Daniel Phillips, Pastor
● Officiating ●

'A Message to DeShawn'
Silent after blunt, ride after ride, we'll hook up on the other side, watch over
your family and your newborn, til we meet again Homie.
From all of your brothers and sisters,
on Cougar Street
We Gia Much Love For You'

Newspaper

Waking up the next morning, I reached out for Deshawn. Silently, I began to weep as I remembered he was gone. Lying in bed, I started wondering where Deshawn was at this very moment. What was being done to him? Had he been flown to Iowa City yet for an autopsy? "It's sad. The first time Deshawn will have flown in a helicopter is when he is dead, awaiting to be cut open and examined." It really is weird what you think about when you lose a man so young and tragically—all that he will miss in a life he never really got to live, all from such a senseless act.

When I finally got up from bed, all I wanted was a newspaper. Andie had already gone out that morning to pick up one at the convenient store. The big step for me was just to look at it. What a heart-wrenching feeling I had. *How does a woman do it?* I thought. *How do I deal with this brutal fatality that happened to a man I cared for and loved? Yet the anger festers inside me toward the world.*

Finally, I just grabbed the newspaper off the end table and glanced at the front page, yet as hard as I could, I threw it down on the floor as papers scattered all around. I just broke down and cried. My man, on the front page of the newspaper, was lying on a stretcher with his blood in detail outlining his body. For all intents and purposes—dead.

My heart began pulsating so fast. How could they put a picture so graphic and in color on the front page? The picture was so detailed with grief; the paramedic's face was an easy giveaway. His face was so saddened and full of emotion, and his eyes swelled up as if he were fighting back his intent to cry. This man left you with a feeling of disbelief and uneasiness.

I just kept thinking, *Don't the people at the newspaper company have any respect or consideration for the ones who were close to him and lost him? How seeing this picture of him would hurt any of us or at least leave us with a haunting image for life that won't go away?* Never did I need to see him like that. Basically, I felt poor judgment was used all to get a front-page story.

Just what reason, what purpose, did this picture have for anyone else who did not know him? It meant nothing to them. Probably just another dead black man.

But this picture meant something to me, and it caused me an abundant amount of grief to look at it. I should have never had to see Deshawn like that. His arms in the picture were folded around his body, and his hands rested on his stomach. Seeing that, I just knew he never had a chance of making it.

After dealing with the dramatic picture that broke me inside, I saw another picture of him that had not much of a resemblance of the man I knew. It was far from being recent. I had never seen Deshawn like that ever. He had a fat face and was wearing glasses. Where did the newspaper get this photo? I didn't know, and neither did his mother. Maybe they were so hard up for a story that anything would do. Beneath his picture, it stated, "Deshawn Price leaves behind a pregnant girtlfriend."

While still trying to get over the first picture, this statement just broke me down. They didn't want to talk to me, but they wanted to let the world know I was pregnant. I started crying so hard; I was feeling so much emptiness and pain. *What am I going to tell my child someday?* I kept thinking over and over in my mind. What hurts the most was, someday when I did tell our child, would I show these newspaper articles and pictures? And if so, when?

Eventually, I began to read the paper, but my mind was not focused on what I was reading. Everything I read did not seem to register, but a few statements did manage to catch my eye.

The Waterloo Courier stated that, "One of their sources said Deshawn was being initiated into a gang when the incident occurred. If the initiate trusts the gang members, he will allow another gang member to pull the trigger on the gun, and he is then reportedly initiated into the gang, the source said."

When I read that, I was angry! I was so angry that I could hurt someone myself, and I was not at all that type of person. If the source was not Deshawn, what could this source really know, and what business did the paper have printing it? This was not factual information, just what one source thought they knew. To be honest, if he was in a gang, that is not what caused his death, I felt. The important fact the journalist seemed to ignore was that he was a human being. He was still someone's son and someone's future husband and soon-to-be father. He never went around stealing or beating people up. Never was he a bad man in my eyes despite his faults. He had a special gift. Deshawn could touch anyone's life with a smile or sweet gesture. He helped people; he had a bleeding heart of compassion and respect for others. Deshawn would give someone his last without any hesitation.

The journalist didn't bother to consider the environment he came from. What he grew up around and what he learned and knew to survive in life out on the streets, was this really all his fault? Partial blame should be brought about to society for not doing anything but criticizing what I feel they started. Not giving a ray of hope or opportunity to these young black men, only taking them down and locking them up.

Deshawn deserved to die with at least some honor and respect instead of being exploited by the media. The media, I felt, were not out to care nor spare feelings, all because of the way he died. That is so judgmental and sad, yet that's our society.

Although I managed to get over the newspaper that morning, I still had a whole day to go through before it was over. I was sitting on the living room floor with my pajamas on and my face puffy from all the tears I've cried. There were so many thoughts running through my mind. Then suddenly, I remembered what Deshawn had told me just before he got out of the car for the last time… He had found a baby crib that he wanted to buy, and now I would never know which baby crib it was. That bugged the mess out of me. It just dug its way underneath my skin—the fact of never knowing.

My mother arrived at the apartment that morning and brought me my own copy of the newspaper. Seeing my mother, my eyes lit up because she was here to comfort me, but at the same time, I got this tight feeling in the back of my throat as my eyes filled with tears. How grateful I was to have her at my side. I never had anyone close to me die before, and no one, not even my mother, could relate to what I was experiencing. What was worse was that I was pregnant and I was scared to grieve and deal with the situation tragically brought upon me in fear of being so emotionally stressed that I would cause harm to my unborn child.

My mother and I were talking, and all I could talk about was how Deshawn had gotten out of the car the day that I dropped him off at his mother's house. I described how he had walked across the street and turned around, looked back at me, and smiled as he waved goodbye; and he never turned around to head toward the house until I started to pull off to go to work. His mother, Katie, said he was smiling and acting so happy that day. I swear there was almost an aura surrounding him, a brightness. I just couldn't stop talking about this. He just never looked at me in quite that way. He had the sweetest smile on his face, and it radiated warmly. Deshawn looked so happy. I console within myself that at least he seemed at peace and full of life that day.

I was so dazed and silent within myself as I lay on the couch, drowning in sorrow. I felt as if I'd been haunted and violated by such a traumatic death. Emptiness was my companion at this present time. What I had to deal with was filling this void of endless time.

I began to look outside the window, when I was alarmed to my recognition that my car was gone. I immediately became hysterical, asking everyone, "Where is my car?" I had no recollection whatsoever. Andie finally calmed me down and told me it was still parked at Walmart's parking lot. I didn't care. I wanted my car sitting outside our apartment building on the street now! That car was Deshawn's baby; he loved my car. Deshawn would clean it two or three times a week. He put $1,500 worth of sound system in the car. He even paid my monthly car payment and insurance. Deshawn would never let the gas tank go below a half of a tank. He thought it was bad for the car. With that car's absence, I felt more of a void.

I kept communicating all morning to whoever was at the apartment about every single memory that came to mind. Reminiscing brought about tears along with laughter. I was finally laughing at the things Deshawn did, but it still hurt inside to dig deep within and bring about these memories and share them, as well as feeling some sense of guilt for having been laughing. I had a notebook and pen that I carried around with me. As I would talk and remember something, I would write it down because I never wanted to forget a thing. I wanted to remember so one day I could share it with our child.

Around eleven o'clock that morning, there was a knock on our door. We weren't expecting anyone, but there in the doorway stood my friends. They had been excused for the day from classes at school because of Deshawn's death and, most of all, to be with me. Once again seeing them, I lost my breath for a moment as I broke down in tears. They were crying along with me as they proceeded into the apartment.

We all gathered around and sat on the living room floor, talking about happier times spent with Deshawn. We were looking back at how we met and the things Deshawn did. Just remembering made us laugh. That's the kind of man he was: full of life and character. Nothing said was ever sad or bad; it was all good, funny, and mostly positive. That was the true Deshawn. A good man.

I met Deshawn all because of some coat. I laughed at just the thought. I had always wanted a black Charlotte Hornets coat, but my mother refused to buy me one for they were not very ladylike. Well, it was in May of 1992. I went to my friend Wendy's house, and in her bedroom lay this coat I had always wanted. She told me they met these guys the other night and the guy let them wear his coat home because it was cold and raining. My exact words were, "Well, he ain't gettin' this coat back. It's mine now!" I wore that coat around all day wherever I went. Later that night, he called Wendy for his coat. I got on the phone and told him, "You are not getting this coat back." Yeah, right. He showed up at the house with some friends for his coat that night.

I fell in love the moment I saw his smile. That night is when there became an us, and believe me when I say, I eventually got the coat I always wanted.

A deadly game

Waterloo teen killed, friend in jail after loaded gun ends game of 'Trust'

By JEFF KART
and ANN LANGEL
Courier Staff Writers

A game with a gun ended in the death of a Waterloo youth Thursday, and the arrest of one of his friends.

DeShawn Tyrone Price, 18, of 415 Cooper St., was playing with a gun with his brother and friends in the basement of his home when the weapon went off, police said.

The bullet hit him in the head, officials said. Price was transported to Allen Memorial Hospital following the 12:10 p.m. incident, where he died a short time later, police said.

Orlando DeJuan Mims, 19, of 315 Lincoln St., was arrested on a complaint of involuntary manslaughter and held in the Black Hawk County Jail in connection with the death.

Witnesses said Price was holding a gun to his head and asked Mims to pull the trigger, according to court documents. Mims then pulled the trigger thinking the gun was unloaded, the documents state.

Police said the youths were playing a game called "Trust," a version of "Russian Roulette" where the gun is placed under the victim's chin, and the trigger is pulled. Trust reportedly is played as a form of initiation. One source said Price was being initiated into a gang when the incident occurred.

If the initiate "trusts" the gang members, he

will allow another gang member to pull the trigger on the gun, and he is reportedly initiated into the gang, the source said.

At Mims's initial court appearance this morning, bond was set at $75,000.

Assistant County Attorney Kim Griffith asked for a $50,000 bond for Mims, but District Associate Judge Thomas Bower set the bond higher, citing Mims' juvenile record and probation status.

Griffith said the shooting was a "very serious offense," adding that Mims pulled the trigger and a bullet went in the victim's head.

She said Mims has an extensive juvenile record, including three second degree burglary charges and an overall, crimes for which he was adjudicated delinquent as a juvenile.

Mims also is currently on probation from Cedar Rapids, Griffith said, for delivery of drugs.

Mims told the judge he works at the Mandian Cafe in downtown Waterloo, making $95 a week.

Involuntary manslaughter is an aggravated misdemeanor, punishable by a maximum two years in prison and a $5,000 fine.

An autopsy on Price was to be performed at this morning at University Hospitals and Clinics in Iowa City, Waterloo Police Chief Bernal Koehrsen said. Dr. Peter Stephans of Cedar Rapids was to perform the autopsy.

Differing accounts from neighbors and family members said the weapon used in the incident was a 9mm or a .380-caliber semi-automatic, although another source said the gun was a revolver.

'It was an accident'

The two youths had known each other since they were about 3 years old, said the victim's mother, Katie Price.

"He was my son's best friend," she said. "but it was an accident, it was a terrible accident. I don't have any hard feelings toward the Mims family."

The mother added, "I hope the law will go easy on him ... I'm deeply sorry it happened.

See SHOOTING / page A3

DeShawn Price
Leaves behind
pregnant girlfriend

Susan Williams, a family friend, reacts to a shooting in her neighborhood Thursday that left DeShawn Price, 18, dead.

29

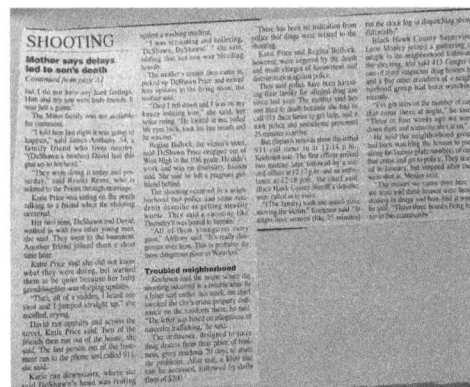

Basement

Opening the door to the basement was one of the most challenging yet fearful things I had to do. I was scared of what my eyes might see as I finally reached the last step of the staircase.

Slowly, I proceeded by placing my right foot on the first step. Holding on to the railing for support, I took a deep breath with the next step I took. My thoughts contemplated how dark and lonely it looked with this feeling of upset in my stomach. Chills ran through my body as my feet were finally planted together on the basement floor. My legs were stiff and trying to hold me back, but I just had to fight this feeling. My eyes focused on the washing machine because when the shooting occurred, that's what he fell back upon as he fell to the floor. I kneeled down beside the washing machine as I placed my hands on the cold, gloomy floor. I then began to caress every area as if Deshawn were still lying there. Specks of blood were hidden within the darkness of this basement floor and the cement was so cold; however, with each touch, I felt my man.

The family had cleaned up the area so I would not witness every gruesome detail, but I searched for any sign or piece of evidence detailing his presence that was left behind. The letters *A*, *B*, *C*, *D* written in white color marked where my man lay, I assume.

A memory appeared in my mind so vividly and gently, yet it was precious to my heart, like a whisper to an ear. This would have been a perfect moment for an "I'm sorry," the Deshawn Price way. There were times in our relationship where we would argue, and Deshawn always knew how to say "I am sorry" with a surprise. At a convenient store, usually on the counter, were ninety-nine-cent roses that are artificial but come in an array of colors and scents. I have so many of these roses, and I love them. Whatever the situation, Deshawn loved to catch me in a perfect moment and present to me a delicate little rose, just to say "I'm sorry," "I love you," or "I was just thinking about you and wanted to let you know." It's such a little gesture, but it's one of the biggest things I cherish and hold on to the most.

At this moment, as I sat and cried alone, I felt some peace and warmth within the core of my being. I found myself just talking out loud to Deshawn. "I love you, Deshawn, and I know you didn't mean to hurt anyone. But you were special and people cared about you. I hurt, Deshawn. I hurt, and I am scared. How can you be gone? I need you. I need you now to hold me, please. Hold me just one last time?" I asked.

I began to fade back in my thoughts to a time when I worked at this place called Taco John's. It was so hot outside that day, and business was slow. I leaned across the counter when in walked Deshawn. My heart raced. I know my face had to be beet red because I was extremely nervous. Deshawn was seeing me in this ugly turquoise-blue uniform, with this oversized Taco John's hat I had to wear, and I was sure I stunk like greasy tacos. But there he was with that smile, walking toward me. All I could think was, *What does this man want? Today I am working with Chip, the meanest supervisor. What will he say to someone stopping by to talk to me?*

Deshawn finally approached the counter and swiped his finger over his top lip as he smiled and pulled out of his pocket a small velvet box and placed it on the counter. I began to shake; I was so nervous. I reached for the box and slowly opened it precautiously. There in this box was a gold ring that said Love in cursive. I said, "Thank you, but I can't believe you came to my job," with a smile on my face. I then placed the box in my pocket. I didn't know how to react; I was beyond nervous.

He then gave me a kiss as he said, "I'll call you later," and he headed out the door. I felt bad that I put the ring in my pocket, but I was dirty from work and I didn't want Chip knowing all of my business. Funny thing is, he never saw one part of my special moment. The good part is, Deshawn knew who I was, and he knew not to take the way I reacted seriously or in a bad way. The man knew he made my day, and that's all that mattered to him. I was surely surprised and happy. He left me completely shaken up. For no special purpose or occasion, I received my first ring. The first one of my life. What was really funny about the situation is that he left the price tag on the ring so I would know how much he had spent. He sure was a character.

When I say I was at peace, I felt like being in that basement where the shooting took place helped me. Maybe Deshawn was there that very moment, and maybe not. Believing in my heart that he was there holding me—that's what gave me peace. I felt in touch with the man I missed so much.

One will never begin to understand what it feels like to kiss the basement floor where my boyfriend was killed. How much I missed him, wanted him, and at the same time, felt bitterness toward him. I felt a feeling of anger from his betrayal he left upon me. I felt like he betrayed me, his responsibilities, our love, and most of all, our unborn child. He left me scared and alone. A single mother I was soon to become because he chose to chance his life to a game called Trust.

I wanted him to be there when the baby arrived. I needed his strength, his support, his hand holding mine coaching me through the delivery, and most of all, *love*. I wanted to have that moment of seeing a proud father's smile as he held the baby for the first time. Now, our soon-to-be-born baby would never get to experience what his father's touch and love feels like.

What was I to do? He left me with the responsibility of being a mother as well as a father. A father—I had no idea how to be. I felt anger as I sat absorbing my thoughts but guilty for feeling this way toward Deshawn. I loved him. Therefore, love holds no grudges. I had to forgive him for doing something so ignorant and for leaving me with a feeling of abandonment because I was not abandoned with God in my life. He is my true strength. I had to realize I would never know and I would have to learn to live with this feeling as well as the question why. I just had to believe it was his time to depart from his life on earth.

He truly was a blessing brought into my life, despite the game he played and his tragic demise.

I cried on my knees that afternoon, thanking God for giving me the chance to know such a giving man. He was wonderful. No one love is alike, and I was truly blessed to have been loved by him. "Thank you, God."

I then kissed the basement floor one last time while watching my teardrops fall and land silently against the floor and, within seconds, fading away. Now this floor not only had a part of Deshawn; it had a part of us—our love ending in sadness that would live forever in this house.

"Deshawn," I whispered, looking down at where he laid, "I want you to know how grateful I am for each day you shared with me. You were always there for me. You saw the best in me, for who I was and the dreams I wanted to achieve. You never held me back, but you helped me keep faith within myself because you believed in who I was. I thank you for being my protector, my inspiration, truly my everything. This bond between us will never be broken, for you will always have a place in my heart, forever and always. Love, to me, will be this one true time in life we shared together, and when I look at our child, I will see nothing but *love*."

Turning my back and walking away, I stopped, looked up to God, and said, "I love you, Deshawn, always." I then wiped my tears from my face. I took a few cleansing breaths and walked up the stairs. I kept telling myself, "Be strong, Melanie, don't cry." Deshawn hated it when I cried. It made him mad. I think he didn't like to see me cry, to see me hurt, because he didn't know how to make everything better. If only he knew he did everything right; he listened and always held me close to his heart.

I took one more breath without turning around. I kept my back to what would be the past. I then shut the door while softly speaking aloud, "Goodbye, Deshawn."

I know being in the basement that day was the best for me. It was the first step to dealing with this lifelong heartbreaking reality. It was the first step out of many to say goodbye, to let go, to deal with the fact of the way he took his life—by trusting friends and playing with a gun. I still wonder if the baby and I crossed his mind at the last moment of his life. If he just thought, What have I done? I pray that he didn't have to end his life with such a feeling or a feeling of immense pain.

I just pray, if anything, that God lets him walk at his child's side, guiding him throughout life.

Emotions and Preparation

As I entered the department store, this song began to play over the speaker. Each word began to speak to my soul. All I could concentrate on was each phrase, as if Deshawn was there communicating with me.

> I miss you, I'm talking to you, baby.
> I miss you.
> We used to talk and laugh all night, girl
> What happened to those days?
> Did they all just fade away?
> Holding you in my arms made me feel so happy.
> Then they say you had to go. What's wrong?

Baby, I need to know.
But now it's a dream that I wish
That you can come back to me.
But you're long gone away
Come on back, babe
I miss you, yes I do.

Deshawn and I loved this song and, most of all, the video. At this moment, I felt I was living it. The video displayed a couple ready to have a baby. Then they showed the mother in the birthing room ready to deliver when they ordered the father to leave as complications occurred. In the end the mother passed away as the baby survived. Finally, they showed the father holding the baby, letting reality really hit you with a feeling of anguish. So I had this video image in my mind as this song played while we were shopping for clothes for Deshawn to be laid to rest in. I tried not to listen to the words, but phrase after phrase had more meaning to me now. I was experiencing a loss in my life, like in the video. In the end, I would be holding our child, alone.

As the song continued, I was occupied with grief.

> I thought you'd be with me
>   forever
> But I guess someone took my
>   place
> Took the place of me loving you
>   and
> Making love to you all through
>   the night.
> I wish you were still here
> So I can see your pretty face again
> Please come back and rescue me
> From all this pain and misery.

While trying to be strong, every phrase invaded my sanity. I just stood still, fighting the urge to cry and trying to help Andie and Regina find the right color and size of pants for Deshawn. Within the store, it was so quiet and empty. Honestly, it gave me a feeling Deshawn was trying to connect with me through this song after hearing it.

> Give me the love back, baby
> The way you used to hold me
> The way you used to kiss me.
> I miss you.
> Every time I lay at night

All I do is cry.
I do love you, baby, I miss you

I lost it! I was screaming frantically, "Why? Why me?" Fresh tears poured from my eyes as I hollered, "I want him back. It's not fair. I miss him." My friend Andie grabbed me and held me compressed in comfort against her chest as she walked me out of the store and into the mall's main area. She found a bench, and we sat down as she just held me and as I kept screaming, "Why did he have to die? He's dead, it's just so final!"

As my face was buried in Andie's hug, I managed to peek through a space in my folded arms as a little girl with her mommy slowly walked by with looks of curiosity. The little girl questioned her mommy with a soft voice, "Why is she crying?" Her mother answered her in a fragile whisper, "I don't know, honey."

A stab of pain shot through my heart. How I loved this man. I had to gain acceptance—all of that and more. Running my hand over my face as my eyes stung, I swallowed hard as I spoke firmly, "I've had enough for today. Can we please go home?" We finished our shopping. I did the best I could, regardless of how painful it was to shop for clothes Deshawn would be buried in.

On the way out to the car, this event today left me with a feeling of, Why am I doing this? But I knew why; because of *love*. Married or not, I had a commitment in my heart to this man that I was driven to see through. What picked at my soul that day while shopping was the fact that Deshawn discussed with me one time what he wished to be buried in if he should die. I never paid much attention to that conversation. I just thought, *Yeah, that is what you would want to be buried in now.* But times change, and so may his wishes. I just never expected death to enter our lives at an early age. This made my day difficult when I couldn't remember what he had told me, except that he wanted to be buried with his lowkes (black sunglasses) on. This is the only detail I remembered. I beat myself up for not listening. I thought it would never happen anytime soon, but it did. It happened too soon.

While we were shopping, I had a decision to make. I could bury him in a suit, except that would not define what and who Deshawn was. I wanted him in something that looked comfortable—an outfit that resembled Deshawn's character and interests in life. The shirt I found was white with a green rectangle in the middle of the shirt with a black Nike swoosh symbol. The store had just gotten these shirts in, and if I bought all of them, no one else would have one. So I purchased a total of eight Nike shirts. One for Deshawn, one for myself, and six for the pallbearers. Next, I bought eight black Nike hats with the white Nike swoosh symbol in the front, only because Deshawn was all about wearing a hat. After purchasing the shirts, we had the lettering RIP printed on the back of each shirt. Then on Deshawn's shirt, we printed Price on the front lefthand corner, and on my shirt, I had Deshawn printed in the front lefthand corner. All that was needed now was a nice pair of black Levi's, Deshawn's favorite.

While walking to the next store I could see my reflection in the glass window of the mall. I got this smirk on my face and let loose a frail laugh as I looked at Andie and Regina. "If only Deshawn could see me now. Finally, my butt is getting bigger. I'm getting a booty!" I smiled delicately as I squeezed my eyes shut, holding back tears. Deshawn used to give me a hard time because I had such a little butt. It was such a funny issue between the two of us. I then released a heavy sigh as I whimpered to myself, "I have to do this."

Entering the department store County Seat, I noticed these silk boxers. "Deshawn loved silk boxers." I felt that Regina could read the expression on my face because with my help, we picked out a pair and she offered to buy. This is when the song "I Miss You" began to play, which had affected the rest of my day.

While in the car, we played the song called "So Alone" by Men At Large. We sang this song out loud together phrase by phrase loudly as tears were shed for this lovely man and our memories together.

So Alone

We were together, just the other day.
Taking life for granted, passing time away.
I was there for you. You were there for me.
We would be together for eternity.
I never knew there be sorrow
But I knew we'd be together tomorrow.
Together, forever,

We were so wrong.
Now I just can't believe that
    you're gone.

Chorus:
And I'm so alone, alone.
You never miss a good friend
    until they're gone.
And I'm so alone. I'm so alone,
    yes, I am.
I really can't believe that you're
    gone, gone, gone.

Life goes on, and it's not the
    same.
'Cause I can't help sometimes
    calling out your name.
But then I realize that you won't
    come around, no.
Oh, what I wouldn't give to see
    your smile.

Oh yes, we've had our ups and
    down
Oh what I wouldn't give to have
    you cussing me out.

I know it sounds funny, but what
     can I say?
My life just ain't been the same,
     since you went away.
Repeat chorus.

See I never knew that there would
     be sorrow
But I knew we'd be together
     tomorrow
Together, forever
We were so wrong, now I don't
     want to believe
I just cannot believe, I really don't
     believe that you're gone.
I'm so alone.

Arriving back at Deshawn's mother Katie's house after a long afternoon of emotional shopping, we entered upon a houseful of guests. A number of people were high or drinking, possibly selling drugs, and others were talking loudly, arguing, as well as grieving. The living room was dimly lit, and I proceeded to sit down on the couch. I began to have an uneasy feeling. Something just didn't feel right. At this moment, we gave all the pallbearers their outfits. Some paid me for them, and the majority did not. They seemed pleased with the idea, except for Deshawn's brother, David, who was going to be difficult and do things his way so he felt more in control. David refused to wear the outfit we had purchased. My mouth dropped wide open as my chest tightened and my heart felt crushed.

Why would anyone feel the need to cause a confrontation over a man's funeral? He gave me an uneasy feeling, as if he was and as if he had an array of anger toward me. As if he was intending to make this situation as stressful for me as he could. It was like he did not like that Deshawn, who was dead, was still getting more attention than him. That's exactly how he presented himself to me. He was looking for a way to pinch a nerve and get your attention and energy focused on him. I just sat still, nostrils flared with anger, along with deep long respirations keeping me from an explosion.

We came to find out the news was about to begin, and David proceeded to become even more peculiar. He would run up the stairs and then down the stairs. The room filled with silence as the ten o'clock news began. David again ran up the stairs fast and then back down. To my surprise, David's face appeared on the television screen with this mischievous grin as he began speaking with a stutter, saying that he'd played this game for years and this was the first accident that had occurred. He said that his brother made a mistake, and he would continue to play considering the odds of how many times he'd played and only once someone had died.

My thought was, *That someone was his brother.* Here everyone knew he was going to be on the news but me, yet no one took offense to what he said but me! The next thing I knew, he ran back up the stairs, smiling like he was a star because he was on TV… We came to find out David kept running up and down the stairs because he was recording himself being on the TV. Did he not know what a fool he looked like and the fool he made others of this family look like? He thought he did something special.

I absolutely could not believe the news station allowed their interview to air on television, possibly just to make them all look bad, because that was my interpretation of the interview. Once again, I began to cry uncontrollably. No one came to Deshawn's defense but me. I stood up and looked at David and said, "How dare you say the things you said? Your brother trusted you and your dumbass game. He's dead now, and you have the nerve to put your smiling ass on TV and say degrading things like it was a joke. If you're so tough and ain't scared to die, why don't you kill yourself? Go play that game again, and I hope you die and prove your own odds wrong!"

David looked at me as he grinned along with a frail laugh and said, "I will."

Everyone looked at me in shock, as I stood there crying, in dire need of some relief. I began to feel really sick from all of the upset. I couldn't feel my baby move, and I began to panic! Everyone gathered around me as Andie volunteered to get me out of there and to the hospital.

While we were in the car, Andie began to lecture me, telling me, "He was wrong to say what he said, but no matter how angry you are, you don't tell anyone you hope they go and kill themselves. You don't *ever* tell anyone to kill themself."

I just looked at her like "whatever." That is how I felt, and I just kept my mouth shut.

Arriving at the hospital emergency room, I was so overwhelmed with what had gone on at Katie's. I was admitted to the labor and delivery room right away for observation. Again, a monitor was placed around my stomach to monitor my baby's fetal heart rate. I felt reassured just to hear the heartbeat once again. I spoke with a doctor about what had gone on and the fact that I can't sleep at night. How I wished for one night of peaceful rest. We continued to wait for the doctor to return when I glanced up toward the door, and to my surprise, my mother began to walk in the door. She walked over to the side of my bed as I asked, "How did you know I was here?"

She said, "Someone from Katie's house called me."

She then sat down, and I explained to her what had gone on. My mother looked at me with tears in her eyes as she spoke hesitantly, "I wrote a poem about the situation." I sat up and smiled. She will never know what that meant to me. I wanted to hear it. I wanted to know what words my mother could possibly find right now to say. She proceeded to pull a piece of paper from her purse and unfolded it very slowly as she read.

> My daughter is a good person
> She was taught by her mother at
>   a very early age
> That all humans deserve to be
>   treated with respect,
> And that life was sacred and to be
>   cherished.

Through the years, as I watched
her grow, society was
changing.
Resulting in the classrooms
becoming more integrated
and students no longer real-
izing color.
As my daughter grew older
One late spring day
Her heart felt a fancy for a young
black man
With a great smile and heart of
gold.
But his foundation was weak
Scarred by dyslexia and other
struggles he encountered
through his childhood.
Consequently he was left with a
powerful feeling of helpless-
ness, inadequacy, and anger.
My daughter, however, knew
another side of this man,
which was kind, gentle, and
loving.
She believed at the core of his
being was a giving man that

helped others, loved her dearly,
And dreamed of their future together.
Despite his hopes, he became a product of his environment.
Which ironically it would lead to his tragic early demise.
As I have struggled with the reality of this senseless act.
I felt disbelief.
While driving in traffic dazed and numb
I have wondered if others could see my pain inside me.
My pain is for a young man
Whose environment and life choices, I fear, left him with a death wish.
Were the obstacles too overwhelming?
My daughter is a sweet, naive young lady
That loved her man.
They loved each other.

They had a forbidden love like
    Romeo and Juliet, and it
    ended just as tragically.
I weep out of sadness for a young
    man
That I believe did not stand a
    chance.
I ask why? I want to ask all of you
    why?
Why was this young man's envi-
    ronment so fatal
He did not deserve to die like
    this, no
He deserved a life of happiness
    with my daughter and his
    child.
He deserved to achieve hopes and
    dreams and to be free from
    the feelings that haunted
    him. (Michelle Clark [my
    mother])

With tears falling gently from my eyes, I was
amazed by the sincere words she had displayed. She
really paid attention to my relationship with Deshawn
and our love for each other. What I needed were

finally some kind words portrayed upon Deshawn with truth. My mom was there for me and gave her daughter what I needed most. What she wrote were "words of art." My mom will never know how much I loved her at that moment and how thankful I am that she is my mother. My mother touched my heart and soul. As we cried together, I decided I wanted this poem to be read at the funeral. I asked my mother if that was all right with her. She said it was but that she felt she could not read it aloud in front of everyone. She stated she didn't want no one to get mad or be offended with what she wrote. I felt it hit the nail on the head; it was all true, completely perfect, and no one had the right to get mad at this poem, I felt. No one spared my feelings with how they felt. I then asked Andie if she would read it aloud at the funeral, and she agreed. I was happy that this poem was going to be shared with others.

As I was lying in the hospital bed, I began to think back to when Deshawn went to my prenatal class with me. We had gone on a tour of the birthing unit, and I remember him making a funny comment about the light that had a few older men laughing. I kept looking at this light above me and more like stared at the light. It may sound funny, but I felt him in that room with me. I know he was with me in more ways than one.

The doctor had returned with an order for a prescription for three pills for three nights to help me get a good night's sleep. The doctor explained that I was far enough in my pregnancy that three pills should not cause the baby any harm. He felt I could use a couple of nights' sleep.

I ended up leaving with my mother as she drove to the twenty-four-hour Osco Drug to pick up my prescription. I waited in the car and rested while she waited inside for the medication to be filled. I watched my mother walk out, and after she got into the car, she handed me a pill and told me to take it now. The pill took effect right away. I don't even remember how I got to bed. Thankfully I ended up with some peace and rest for a night.

*****

Two days later...

We were scheduled to meet at Sanders Funeral Home an hour early for the family viewing of the body before it was to be opened for the public viewing all day. Today was the day I finally could be with

Deshawn. I felt so overwhelmed. It had been over five days since I last touched him and had his presence near. I longed for this day to come, and it was finally here.

I looked out the window at my car and smiled. I hadn't driven my car since Deshawn's death; in fact, I hadn't gone near it. That was one step I was not ready to face, so I got a ride with Andie and Maurice. When we arrived at the funeral home, I was so ready to see my man.

As we walked in, I spotted the casket directly at the other end of the room. I first signed the guest book and then slowly started approaching my man that lay at peace in his casket. I have always feared dead bodies, but this time, the fear did not haunt me. Deshawn's presence gave me some security. When I reached Deshawn, tears gently fell upon my face. I then handed a man the Nike hat I had bought for him. He was so happy that we had brought a hat to cover up any sign of his demise, considering the way he died. He gently placed the hat on Deshawn's head. I then looked at Deshawn and held his hand, as I softly whispered "I love you," placing my lips onto his, for this would be one of our last kisses shared together. However, a dead body can't kiss back.

I then got into my bag and pulled out a picture of the two of us together and placed it upon his hands that were embraced together, as well as one of those artificial flowers that was blue, his favorite color; and I placed the flower up against the picture. This was it. I closed my eyes and prayed. When I opened my eyes, I just looked at this precious man. He looked very well considering where he had been shot at. They did a wonderful job preparing him for viewing. How grateful I was. His face was fatter than usual, but I assume it was the embalming fluid that aided in giving his face more structure. The eyes were sewn shut, and his eyelashes were as curly as ever. His lips appeared to be sewn shut, but his hands seemed to be glued together, very nicely, I may add. It left a peaceful image within my mind. Deshawn's fingernails were so long. That one part of Deshawn I loved was his hands. I stood there, placing my hand on his and feeling how the cold radiated from his skin, how lifeless he was with no spirit—just a cold body portraying death.

Deshawn did look really good, especially in the outfit we bought. He looked comfortable, like my goofy Deshawn. All that was missing was his delicate smile and that sparkle gleaming in his eyes, revealing life!

I then glanced around him at the flowers that had been sent. I read each card, and the last one I read was from Walmart. Tears poured from my eyes at this sweet gesture. I hadn't even started working there yet. This was such kindness that touched my heart. Afterward, I went back over to Deshawn, when someone brought me a chair as I sat at his side. Regina and Katie left that morning after the family viewing to go have their hair done, and eventually, everyone else left too. Myself, I was determined to stay all day, for the next time I would see Deshawn would be at his funeral briefly. And afterward, only in my dreams. That day, I sat at his side, talking to people and sharing pictures and memories of our time together. Later that afternoon, my mother showed up with my aunt. As we were talking, Andie had brought me a tray of food to eat. I was so hungry and thankful. The family knew that I was not leaving my man's side. My appetite had diminished abundantly since Deshawn's death. I was hungry and I tried to eat, but it was just not pleasing. I could barely eat.

Katie and Deshawn's sister Regina showed back up at the funeral home. They had purchased a special flower arrangement on a heart-shaped pillow. It was very nice, but after placing it on his casket, they left again. That night at around seven o'clock, I had to leave. I didn't want to turn my back and walk out the door. I didn't want to say goodbye. I just wanted to curl up next to him and hold on to him so tight. I looked down at Deshawn as I began to weep. It felt so weird being pregnant and looking down at my baby's father lying in a casket with no more life instilled within him. He was at rest peacefully and looked heavenly. I placed my hand once again upon his and gently kissed his lips proudly once again while whispering "I love you." I then turned around and cried as I exhaustedly walked out the door, feeling indulged with melancholy. This was unfair. Finally, I had found my happiness, and then it slipped away before my eyes. My spirits were crushed, and as weird as it may seem, the smell of embalming fluid began to haunt me.

Funeral

The snow lightly fell as the wind slapped against my face, leaving a sting. My tears froze while my stomach turned, leaving me nauseated as I waited outside the church, awaiting Deshawn's funeral. I look around at others as their pain showed through. I have never seen men so sick from grief. They kept quietly to themselves with sunken shoulders, bowed heads, and skin toned with melancholy. Their eyes were inflamed with pain as falling tears revealed that they're only human.

Warm kindness was revealed through many with their hugs, kisses, and soothing words of condolences. I stood numb, eyes glossy from holding back tears as I embraced these kind gestures. I'm blank within my mind. There but not there. Sluggishly, I stood, and silent I remained.

The doors of the church slowly opened, welcoming all. Hesitantly, the crowd formed within the church as others continued to appear with passing time. I assumed my role as I sat in the front pew with immediate family. I could feel eyes fixed on me as feeble whispers revealed my identity: "She was his girlfriend. She is pregnant." Silently still I remained as I listened and watched others around me. I concentrated on his mother, who was dressed so beautifully. She wore an elegant black hat to match her black dress. I loved this lady so much and the strength she radiated as I knew she was drowning inside with grief. She held her son after he was shot while he was gasping for breath and bleeding all over as his friends fled the scene, leaving him alone. Sadness within her was covered up by her appearance and tagged with a weak smile. Tenderly, she was there for me as she made sure I was included in everything and that I sat in the front pew along the side of my mother as family.

I then began to focus on Deshawn's other sister Louise, who at the time was incarcerated yet was allowed to attend her brother's funeral. She was dressed in what appeared to be in a clean-pressed navy-blue dickey suit. She was balling her head off with tears profusely running. Her hands were locked down in handcuffs, and her feet were planted to the floor as shackles were in place around her ankles, preventing her from any type of escape. Along with her stood a prison guard whose eyes were planted directly on her.

To my recognition, I came upon a man I had never met before until this morning before we arrived at the church. This man was dark black, short in height, with curly eyelashes and long strong fingernails just like my man. He resembled such great features Deshawn had. That morning, I found out he was Deshawn's real father. This came directly as a surprise, for the man I knew as Deshawn's father was just his stepfather. Neither Deshawn nor his family ever mentioned this man. This man was never around until today. "A little late," you'd think I would say, but I didn't. Anytime is better to show up than not at all. It took enough out of him, I'm sure, to show up today since he never was there in his life that I was aware of. That had to be hard enough. I embraced him with a warm heart and a soft smile.

I glanced at the funeral service brochure. Deshawn's picture was on the front page. My finger traced the outline of his image. I remained lost in the only images I've got. I began to read the message to Deshawn:

> Blunt after blunt, ride after ride, we'll hook up on the other side. Watch over your family and your newborn, til we meet again, homie. From all your brothers and sisters on Conger Street. We got much love for you!

Sweltering tears overflowed in my eyes as I held my breath, shaking my hand and taping my foot while trying to fight this intense pain. I exhaled, fighting back tears with everything I got, but failed. I was wiping away the tears, using up every tissue I had as others generously contributed, passing more Kleenex my way.

Pastor Danial T. Phillips was about to start when my mother tightly embraced my arm as she looked into my eyes and smiled. I just felt gut-wrenchingly awful. Everyone around appeared neatly done up, and as for me, my hair was a mess. I didn't have the strength nor the spirits to fix it up. My makeup revealed a weak attempt to cover up my weeks' worth of grief. For the pale tone shown through. Noticeable was the loss of weight I was unable to hide. I was emotionally sick to sit here and know I lost my best friend, my special companion. I was empty. Anyone could look at me and read me. When the funeral was over, we did not proceed to a direct burial. I am not sure why. I assume due to money and other circumstances.

Family and Friends

My mother revealed that my father told her to "get her home now! Haven't you heard of Romeo and Juliet?" This meant so much to me. Our relationship had been tainted for years as I was attracted to and dated black men. Deshawn was black. My father had a hard time accepting our relationship and love for one another due to the color of his skin. However, he was willing to take the first step and look past his feelings and what he had been taught throughout life and have me move home. This was the first step of many to rekindle our father-daughter relationship. I moved home to be with the love of family, to grieve, to feel safe, and to get back on my feet and move forward in life when the time was right.

I dropped out of high school. There was no way I could go back and face everyone while pregnant and grieving. I got my GED in a matter of days when I was ready; however, I was ashamed I had to do this. There were many choices I didn't want to make. My life got knocked off course, and with the love of my family and friends, I eventually found my way back. Thank you for your love and support.

Stages of Grief

Now I have painted a picture of a true real-life experience, and I portrayed a lot of feelings one goes through with grief. "The stages of grief are: 1.) Denial and shock 2.) Anger 3.) Bargaining 4.) Guilt 5.) Depression 6.) Loneliness 7.) Acceptance 8.) Hope. Everyone goes through all these stages, however, not always in this order" (Death and Grief, p.2).

I blamed myself, thinking, *If only I was there, this would have never happened.* I was in denial and shock; it felt like he was just on a vacation. I was in shock by the way he died and that he was dead. I was very angry, lonely, and depressed for a very long time. I wanted to block things out, and I honestly think that is a survival method I learned that has affected the rest of my life. I block things out and don't remember a lot like I once did. I also question a lot of things in life now.

Learning from my own experience, I know there are ways to deal with death and grief. These are some of the things I did that others can use:

1. Learn about religion and about God.
2. Learn how to pray or speak to the universe or whatever you believe in.
3. Journal—writing things down is a great way to get things out and heal.
4. Check out books from the public library on death and grief. It's a great source of knowledge to help with understanding and to form your own beliefs.
5. Read quotes. I began to read and collect quotes to get me through different emotions and stages of life.
6. Talk—it hurts at first, but the more you talk, the better you deal with the situation, aid yourself in healing, and be able to move forward. Talk to a counselor, a parent, a friend, or just someone you can talk to.
7. Visit the grave or the site of the death, if possible. Talk out loud to your loved one. Just do it; it really does help.

8. Write everything down that you can remember. You will be surprised years later how much you can forget or block out, and it is nice to have to look back and remember.

9. Allow yourself to cry and grieve and deal with death. Don't hide; you hurt yourself more.

10. Watch inspirational movies, sermons, or documentaries on TV and YouTube. You begin to relate, and it makes you believe in something, have hope, and feel better.

11. Give yourself time to heal; don't rush it.

I also visited the scene of the crime. I went into the basement where he was shot. It was a chance out of many to say goodbye. My unborn child was another source of hope to survive. It took me about two years to grieve enough before I was ready to start moving forward in life as far as getting out and socializing and eventually dating. Deshawn's death also changed my expectations for my life; I wanted better for myself. Still at times, I have a day or two every year when I think of Deshawn, and it really bothers me to my core all day long, especially if I dream about him, as the dreams always seem so real.

Life always presents challenges, but God is never so unkind as to not also bring about solutions to the challenges brought on in our lives. That's life—the good and the bad. The ying-yang. Learn from life and try to be a better human to yourself and others. When you love someone, you don't want to let go; it is extremely hard to move forward. They were a major part of your life. Yet if you don't heal and move forward, it will hold you back. It will cut you off from living your life, which can affect your health and well-being. You have to learn to live again while keeping their memory alive.

These are the things I did through the years:

1. Talk to a counselor.
2. Check out books from the library.
3. Talk to friends and family or anyone that would listen. Find a support group.
4. Carry a pen and paper and write down every memory you can think of.
5. Start a scrapbook.
6. Read and remember quotes.
7. Start a gratitude journal or any kind of journal.
8. Do affirmations.
9. Start painting.

10. Surround yourself with positive things.
11. Believe they would want the best for you and use that as fuel to feed your energy to keep going and achieve.
12. Pray or start a prayer journal.
13. Save important things.
14. Go to church.
15. Do yoga.
16. Meditate.
17. Buy crystals.
18. Go out in nature. Take a walk. Take off your shoes and ground yourself with the earth.
19. Hug a tree.
20. Do aromatherapy.
21. Do acupuncture.
22. Do massage therapy.
23. Do Reiki.
24. Do art of any kind
25. Listen to music.

Baby

I woke up to horrific cramping, mostly in my back. It felt like period cramping that got worse and worse over time. I lay in a fetal position, rocking back and forth on my knees, taking in the pain. I was thinking, *I've got to be in labor! Today is the day I've been scared of yet waiting for.* My contractions were five minutes apart at around 4:00 or 5:00 p.m. that day. I was home with my father as my mother was at work. In a state of panic, I didn't know what to do. I don't think I said much to my father. I called my friend who picked me up to take me to the hospital. On the way to the hospital, I kept thinking, *Today is June 16th. I cannot have my baby on the sixteenth. Deshawn died on the sixteenth of March.*

I remember lying in the hospital bed, ready to push. I focused on the bright light above me. With the energy from this light, I felt Deshawn was there with me. I felt his presence, his energy, in the room that very moment. My mother was by my side. She was scared but continued to hold my hand and coach me through the delivery. After about an hour of pushing, my beautiful baby boy was born at 2:07 a.m. on June 17, 1995. He had a head full of dark-black curly hair, weighing seven pounds, one ounce, and twenty inches long. I felt the emotions of happiness, gratitude, and love mixed with emptiness, sadness, and hope. This was the best day of my life, yet his father was absent from this moment we longed to share together. I felt shattered that he would never get to hold his son in his arms. Yet I was comforted by holding our son. I was holding "our love" and what our love for one another created. He was my strength to move forward and survive the tragedy of losing his father. My baby was a gift from God. I felt truly blessed.

There was no doubt or question in my heart. I named our son after his father. May God allow his father to walk by his son's side throughout life, guiding him on this journey called life.

Birth Certificate

The most important thing to me was having Deshawn Price named as the father on his son's birth certificate. I was told the only way Deshawn could be named as the father on our son's birth certificate was to appear before a judge. How would I prove he was the father? He was dead.

I did just that then. I appeared before a judge and made a request to have Deshawn Price named as the father on the birth certificate. Deshawn's mother, Katie, wrote a note explaining her son was the father. I brought the death certificate with me along with the newspaper article that stated, "He leaves behind a pregnant girlfriend." I just hoped and prayed for a positive outcome.

The judge just shook his head and was in disbelief that I had to appear before him to have Deshawn

Price placed as the father on our son's birth certificate. The judge was very kind, and with no fight at all, he granted Deshawn Price be added as father to the birth certificate of his son. Thank you, God!

David

David is Deshawn's older brother who was playing the game called Trust on March 16, 1995, that tragically killed his brother. He got on the local news and said his brother made a mistake that day and that he would continue to play the game called Trust.

The day Deshawn died, in the newspaper, you could see David in the police car with his hands covering his face while they wheeled Deshawn by him on the stretcher, outlined in blood. David first took the blame and said he was responsible for shooting Deshawn even though Deshawn's best friend, Orkey, shot him. Why did David take the blame at first? Was there more to this tragedy no one would know except for the men in the basement? To this day, no one in that basement that day has spoken of the tragic event in detail. No one has explained what really happened. What is the truth?

David, to me, is guilty of something. I have always felt it in the pit of my stomach by his behavior. His behavior was never of sorrow but of evil. He fought me every step of the way, and I really have no clue why. After the death of Deshawn, I moved out of our apartment and back home with my parents. I had not moved everything out of the apartment yet as I was pregnant and didn't think there was such a rush. That was my mistake as David took our television out of our apartment. He just felt he had the right to Deshawn's television that Deshawn purchased for our family. It took months, but Deshawn's mother, Katie, got it back for Deshawn's son. Honestly, if there was something he wanted of his brother's, all he had to do was ask.

I filed a claim at the courthouse for the seized property of Deshawn Price. This pretty much was about the clothes he was wearing that day he died. David Price found out I filed a claim, and he, as well, filed a claim for his brother's belongings. I received a letter in the mail informing me that "David's claim was denied and The Court has been advised that the property at issue in this case has either been returned or will be returned to the descendant's mother without a formal court order." After Katie received Deshawn's belongings in a large paper brown sack, she gave them to me.

Then one day in the kitchen at Katie's house, David verbally attacked me for giving Deshawn Jr. the last name Price. Price was his last name, not his brother's father's last name. However, Price was the last name of his mother, Katie, and of Deshawn on his birth certificate and death certificate. I couldn't believe this conversation was occurring. Why did David have such a problem with this? Why was he threatened by it? Why was he angry I gave our son the last name Price? All I did was name our son after his father.

I knew about the fear Katie Price had regarding my son being around her son David Price. I couldn't bring little Deshawn around when Uncle David was around because Katie had some fear David would hurt him. What did she know that I didn't? What gave her this feeling? Why did I also have this gut feeling and fear that David would hurt my son if given the opportunity?

Regarding Deshawn's headstone, everyone contributed money to get Deshawn a headstone. Even myself, I gave $150 toward his headstone. I did not know David was the one who chose his headstone and what was to be written on his headstone. I cannot believe the disrespect. The headstone read:

> Deshawn T. Price
> NO TRUST
> May 9, 1976–March 17,1995
> GDLT FCHSUE

No TRUST—are you fucking serious? Deshawn trusted his brother and friends with his life and played a game and died. Then GDLT is for Deshawn, meaning Gangster Disciple Looney Tunes, and the FCHSUE is David's gang, Four Corner Hustler and I don't remember the rest.

Why would David put his gang stuff on his brother Deshawn's headstone? The pain this has caused was such disrespect in my eyes. Why? I just will never know or understand why. It caused anguish and humiliation. It's a constant reminder of that day and how his brother feels about his own brother every time we visit Deshawn's grave.

In December 1997, I received a call that David Price was at Allen Hospital. He tried to hang himself in the Black Hawk County Jail with a sheet. I visited the family at the hospital. I went into the hospital room of David Price. He was lying naked with a sheet over him in the hospital bed. There was this white lady with blondish-white hair I'd never met before. I believe she played bingo with Katie and was in the room with David when I entered. Out of nowhere, she said out loud to me, "We all thought he would have done this a lot sooner."

I was in shock! I was thinking to myself, *What did she just say to me? Why did she say this? Why does she feel this way?* I kept quiet and kept to myself, not knowing what to say or how to feel.

This lady then said to me, "Tell him who you are, talk to him, and say your goodbyes."

I began to say, "David, it's Melanie." Immediately, David then began to have a seizure, and I had to exit the room. I never got to say goodbye, nor did I need to. David Price died on December 17, 1997.

I almost did not go to David's funeral. I had my own personal reasons for feeling like he killed my Deshawn or had more to do with his death than I will ever know. At the last minute, my friend Andie talked me into attending his funeral. Seeing David in the casket made me sick, traumatized, and full of dread. David did not look like David. He did not look good the way Deshawn looked at his funeral. Maybe it was from the way he died. I really have no idea, except it hurt to see him like this. Before I was about to exit the church, Reverend Danial T. Phillips stopped when he got to me, looked at me straight in my eyes as if looking into my soul, and leaned in and gave me the biggest sympathy hug. Why? I've always wondered why he did that as just two years prior, he was the pastor of Deshawn's funeral.

A lot of people believe the Waterloo Police killed David Price, that there is no way someone can kill themselves in the Black Hawk County Jail. There was a lawsuit, and money was awarded to David's children. However, I believe otherwise. I believe in my heart that David was smart and crazy enough. I believe that his guilt got to him, and I believe he found a way to kill himself.

Breast Cancer at Twenty-Four Years Old

In October 2002, while taking a bath, I felt a small BB-sized lump in my upper right breast. Thoughts raced in my mind. Days went by, and this small lump remained. *It's probably nothing but...*

On October 25, 2002, I had an ultrasound of my right breast done. The right breast ultrasound results read: there are two solid round hypoechoic 5–6 mm nodules, 12 o'clock right breast superficially corresponding to the palpable lump. These are non-specific, and biopsy is suggested.

In November 2002, I met with the surgeon and he performed a needle biopsy. When the results were in, he explained the results showed not enough cells. The surgeon then went on to say, "You are so young.

I doubt you have cancer. If the lump bothers you, I can remove it."

After I had time to think about it, I trusted my gut feeling and decided to have the lump removed.

On November 22, 2002, I was brought to an outpatient surgical area then into a minor procedure room where the nodule was removed. I was then informed they would contact me with the results when they received them. Days went by, and I heard nothing from the surgeon. I was hopeful, taking it as a good sign, since no news is good news.

On December 2, 2002, I received a call from the surgeon's office. They wanted to see me the very next day, December 3, 2002, to discuss my biopsy results. When I hung up the phone, I knew I had breast cancer. Fear and worry tormented my mind. All I could think was, it took weeks to get in to see this surgeon, and now they want to see me the very next day.

On December 3, 2002, I was diagnosed with invasive ductal breast cancer to my right breast at the age of twenty-four years old. I was shocked to hear this diagnosis. What? How? They ask you if you have any questions. *I don't know! I haven't had time to digest the fact I have breast cancer. I have no idea what to ask at this very moment,* I thought. I did bring up that I now felt another lump on my right breast. It was discussed, and another biopsy of this new lump would be scheduled.

On December 16, 2002, while entering the outpatient surgical minor procedure room with my mother and fiancé with me, we started asking the surgeon questions regarding my diagnosis. He was in a rush, frustrated and bothered with all the questions we were asking, so we stopped asking questions. I was awake during this procedure like the last procedure, but this time, the surgeon was rough and burned me with the electrocautery machine more than once. I immediately started crying. I was frightened. I was dealing with so much worry and wonder about what was next, and currently this man was hurting me as if I was no one. When the procedure was over, the surgeon explained they would send the biopsy off to the lab for evaluation. Again, he stated, "You're young, I doubt it's anything to be worried about."

I thought, *Are you serious? I was just diagnosed with breast cancer, but you think this biopsy now is nothing.* I was emotionally distraught. How could he treat me like this? Was he clueless?

With my face red and still crying, a nurse approached me and my family afterward and stated, "I could get in trouble for saying this and lose my job, but this surgeon is new and young. Get her to Mayo Clinic!" When we left that day, I made an appointment immediately with my doctor to be referred to Mayo Clinic for a second opinion.

On December 18, 2002, the second biopsy of the right breast results read "Invasive ductal adenocarcinoma. Nottingham grade 2 (of 3), forming a mass 0.5 cm in diameter. The first biopsy was a Nottingham grade 1 (of 3) forming a nodule measuring 0.6 cm. Immunostains for estrogen and progesterone receptors are positive."

On December 30, 2002, and January 8, 2003, at the Mayo Clinic, recommendations of a simple mastectomy and SNL biopsy were suggested. I, the patient, wished for prophylactic bilateral mastectomy and immediate reconstruction. Why? My reasoning for this decision was that I was so young—just twenty-four years old, and I felt my chances of the breast cancer returning were great due to my age. If it were to come back, I may not be as lucky and catch it early enough. A bilateral mastectomy reassured me that I had done all that I could to prevent a recurrence or, even worse, prevent death at an early age. The goal was surviving.

On January 16, 2003, I met with the plastic surgeon regarding my decision for a bilateral mastectomy with reconstructive surgery. This team was so gentle to my needs and concerns. I finally felt I was in the right hands and I would be taken care of by the best. It was discussed that this was a two-year or longer journey. I would require multiple surgeries, even nipple reconstruction. This information was a lot to process, and I was not sure if I understood it all. But choices had to be made fast, and this was now a new chapter of my life I must conquer. Surgery was scheduled for January 21, 2003.

Now the hardest discussion I would have was with my son. How would I explain I had cancer and there was a chance I could die?

Bilateral Mastectomy

Mayo Clinic Notes: Ms. Clark discovered breast cancer in her right upper breast on self-examination. She had biopsies that showed invasive ductal carcinoma. She will require a bilateral mastectomy with a right simple mastectomy and sentinel lymph node biopsy as well as left simple mastectomy alone on the left. Unless the lymph nodes are positive, she will not require radiation therapy. She is very thin, weighing ninety pounds.

January 21, 2003. Today was the day. I was so nervous with my family at my side. They asked if I would like a nun to come and say a prayer for me. *It can't hurt,* I thought. *I need all the prayers I can get.* Regardless of my family at my side, I felt so alone. I was very emotional inside, trying not to cry, and was completely alone with my thoughts and fears that I chose to keep to myself. I truly was alone, for no one in the room would know what it was like to be so young and lose a part of their womanhood. I was terrified.

I do not remember much about this day or even the week. I assume it's due to pain medication, and maybe it's easier to block it all out. I do know that my lymph nodes tested negative for cancer. I was able to have my Becker implants/expanders placed behind my chest wall. I had to have tubes placed inside of me on each side of my body, which I could feel. This was because weekly, we would slowly fill the ports with normal saline to slowly expand the breast muscle. I also had four drain tubes, two on each side of my breast that hung from my body with bulbs on the end of each tube to collect the draining blood. What a sight!

I remember that after surgery, I needed to empty my bladder, and I told the nurse I think she needed to call the cath team to come and empty my bladder via catheter. This nurse refused for a moment and felt I needed to get out of bed and try to use the restroom. I told this nurse, "If I could pee right now in this bed, I would, but I can't pee!" She then called the cath team.

After emptying my bladder via catheter, the nurse stated, "I guess you did need to use the bathroom. You had a liter of urine in your bladder."

All I could think to myself was, *No shit, I know my body.* But I refrained from saying anything else to her. This is something that can happen after being put under anesthesia—the bladder can be slow at regaining its ability to empty the bladder.

That whole week was a blur. I remember my mother and brother visiting one day. My fiancé was there with me for the week, but I don't remember him really being there with me. Honestly, he wasn't around much at all, his excuse being that he didn't like hospitals. The worst part was, he had my cell phone the entire time. I was all alone.

For my first shower at home, I cried. I cried hard. The feeling in my breasts was gone. It hurt, feeling like needles were poking my breast when the water hit them. The biggest reality I wasn't prepared for was that my nipples were gone! My body image was tainted. I felt robbed of my womanhood from breast cancer. I fell to the floor of the shower, on my knees, my face buried in my hands, and crying uncontrollably while the water hit my body. Again, I was all alone.

The beginning of my journey. During my time of healing, this consumed a lot of rest. I couldn't even pick up a gallon of milk. My drain tubes had to be drained four times a day. When they drained only five cc to ten cc of blood a day, then they could be removed. I was weak, trying my best to fight and to heal. The painful part was, once a week my implants had to be filled with normal saline. I was able to have a friend learn how to do this so it could be done at home. A needle was injected into the port on each side of my body. Once the needle was in, she would pull back, and if you saw the blue color, you were in the correct spot and the implants could be filled. There were times I was poked multiple times before she was in the correct spot. I can't express enough how much I hated this part. Sleeping was uncomfortable for me as I had new boobs that didn't move, just as stiff as a rock, and I could feel the tubing inside my body when lying down. Getting comfortable was very difficult and almost impossible. I'm sure I was depressed; who wouldn't be?

I was mostly stuck in the house for weeks. It was difficult going anywhere with four drain tubes and finding clothing I could stuff them in to hide.

Family and friends were around; however, life doesn't stop for them when life is in a standstill for yourself. They still had a life to live and bills to pay. Plus, there was only so much a person really could do for me. All my fiancé did was work and go out to the bar—not the best love and support I needed. Again, I was alone, fighting to survive.

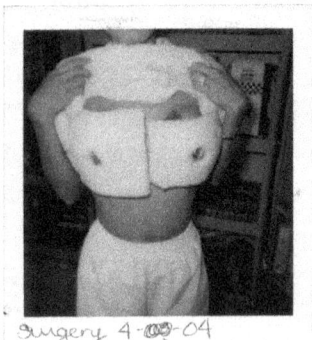

surgery 4-00-04
Date 4-14-04

surgery wed 4-00-04
date 4-14-04

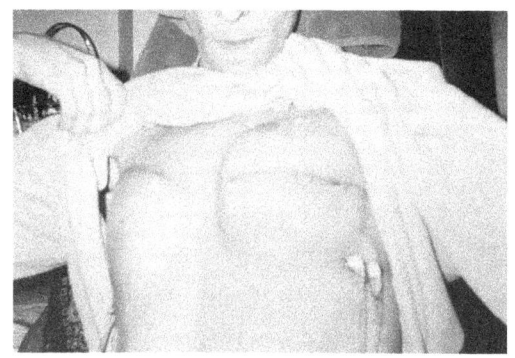

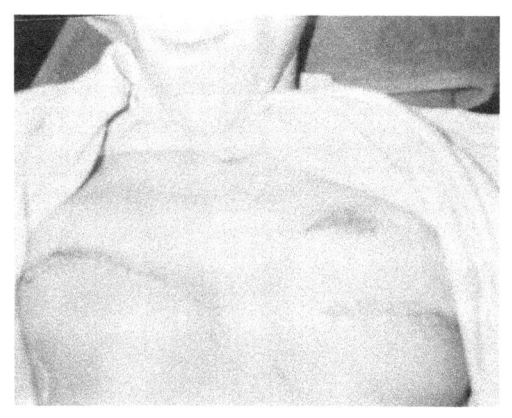

Hope

I missed my period and was throwing up all the time, and I was healing from a bilateral mastectomy at twenty-four years old. My body was so fragile and weak. How could this be? I was pregnant! Now what?

It appears I went into surgery for a bilateral mastectomy while a day or two pregnant. All I could think was, *What a blessing. Another piece of me to live on if I don't make it.* I refused to abort the pregnancy if need be. I would choose the baby to survive over myself. This was my choice, and I made it prior to seeing my doctor.

Options had been discussed with my family doctor. I could do chemotherapy around six months into my pregnancy or wait until after the baby was born. I had decided to wait until the baby was born.

My son, Deshawn, and this unborn child were my fight to survive, my motivation.

I had more than morning sickness. I threw up all the time. This pregnancy was so different from my first pregnancy, except both were occurring at traumatic times in my life. I just knew and had hoped I was having a healthy baby girl.

Marriage

Terry, my fiancé, decided we were getting married in one week. The date was set for August 1, 2003. He decided we would get married in my mother's backyard by his mother's pastor.

Now if you know Terry, he would say and plan a lot, but most of the time, he didn't follow through. It was just talk or good intentions. I just didn't know how to feel or what to believe. I was still healing from my mastectomy and reconstruction from breast cancer, along with being pregnant and a few months away from delivering. Honestly, I didn't believe we were getting married just like that in one week. Yes, we were engaged. I was six and a half months pregnant, and he made the comment of wanting to do things the right way by being married before our baby was born. But I just didn't believe him!

Days before August 1, 2003, I realized Terry was serious. We applied for a marriage license. *I already have a white dress that is brand-new I could wear if, and I mean if, this is really happening,* I thought to myself. Now we were a day or two before the wedding day, and I needed a maid of honor. My best friend Tina was out of town, making her unavailable, so Terry called my other friend Tracey to see if she would be my witness/maid of honor. She was available and agreed. Whose fiancé does that, calling your friends to be a witness to our wedding? He just took control of everything.

August 1, 2003

It was actually happening! I was in a state of panic and full of doubt. *Am I doing the right thing?* I knew deep down inside this was a mistake. This was not how I wanted to ever get married. I didn't even plan a thing. Terry made all the plans and arrangements. It was all happening at the last minute at such a rush—why?

My son, Deshawn, was out of town in Hammond, Indiana. I didn't understand the urgency of getting married. He should be here! Since my son would not be able to attend the wedding, Terry agreed his children would not attend. Deshawn Jr. was actually in Indiana at my ex-boyfriend's mother's house, visiting since we all remained close. The only close family I had at my wedding was my mother, aunt, grandmother Wilma, and my friend Tracey that I can remember. However, Terry had his mother, father, all of his brothers and sisters, cousins, and an array of aunts and uncles, along with his close friends and his daughters at our wedding. I felt horrible; he lied to me! Terry was good at putting me in situations like this. I felt stuck. My son should be here. I failed…

I was in a state of panic. I was in the bathroom with my friend Tracey, crying and freaking out! I was so emotional; I was hiding in the bathroom, pregnant, smoking cigarettes, and trying to calm my nerves. I knew in my heart this was wrong. I knew Terry was a liar and a cheater, and as much as I hoped he would change if we got married, I knew he wouldn't change. Maybe it was easier to settle; I knew what to expect. I was good at blocking things out. However, in my heart, the day I said I do, I knew one day we would end in divorce. Who else but me thinks that and knows that feeling on the day of their wedding day!

I was scared to let everyone down, so I let myself down instead. I was always making sacrifices for everyone but myself. *When did I become so weak?*

This was supposed to be the happiest day of my life, yet in my heart, at the core of my being, I was saying I do to the wrong man.

I had breast cancer, had recovered from a bilateral mastectomy, and was currently pregnant. A lot of my friends were already married, and I wanted to be married too. What if my breast cancer were to come back? What if this was it and death was knocking at my door? At least I was married and I had a husband who loved me in the best way he could.

A'marie

The contractions were intense. It was a new level of pain I never felt before! For my first labor with my son, I had back labor pains. This was front labor pain, and I didn't like it. It was almost unbearable. The pain was so bad, the doctor had an oxygen face mask on. Not sure why exactly. I probably was dramatic and hyperventilating, or maybe it was used to calm my ass down.

My mother, for once in my life, was missing from my side as she was currently living in Mexico. She was my mother, and for once, she wasn't present. I was without her at a pivotal moment in my life. I'd never been without her. My husband, at my side, made sure to call my mother to provide comfort and make her a part of our special moment the best way he could. Terry called my friend up to the hospital, along with his family. Terry was a great supporter. He held my hand, held my leg when it was time to push, and coached me through the breathing and all. He even managed to get pictures of the birth. I couldn't have asked for more. My husband blessed me with love and compassion. I was so proud of him. It was a memorable birthing experience.

On October eleventh, our beautiful, precious baby girl arrived into the world. She had a head of black curly hair. Terry cut the umbilical cord and was a proud father. Terry and I liked the name A'marie, and his mother and I liked Gissele. When I held this precious baby girl in my arms, she looked and felt like an A'marie. She is a gift from God!

Months after having A'marie, I decided against having chemotherapy. I believed I did the most drastic measure by having a bilateral mastectomy. I felt in my soul this was the right choice for me.

Change Is Coming

Being proud was an understatement when I bought a house—a home for my family in 2004. It was a beautiful three-bedroom two-bath home with vaulted ceilings. It had a large backyard; not to mention, my neighbors behind me had horses in their backyard. I felt so accomplished. I worked so hard for this. I did it!

Next, we bought a family pet for our new home—a cute petite yorkie puppy we named Princess. Along with a riding lawn mower for our large backyard. I never in my life saw a man that loved to mow the lawn like Terry on his riding lawn mower. It was my family and our home and the memories we would make. I was happy, yet things began to change drastically.

I was pregnant again! My husband was a car salesman and worked ten- to twelve-hour days, and then his brother owned a bar. And every night after Terry was off of work, he would go to work at his brother's bar until 2:00 a.m., 4:00 a.m., and every once in a while, he wouldn't come home at all. This took a toll on me, on our marriage, and I'm sure, on our children. The stress I endured was unbearable.

One night, Terry started cooking hamburger helper on the stove. I was furious. I told him, "I can't take this anymore. Go cook food at whoever's house you've been staying at." I then picked up the pot and started dumping it in the kitchen sink as noodles landed all over the floor and as Terry was trying to stop me from pouring it out.

Terry was on the phone with his dad, screaming, "This bitch just burnt me!" I did not burn Terry at all. Next the police, Terry's sisters, and Terry's father were at my house.

I had called my father and told him, "Terry called the police on me. Please hurry. I need you."

I was on the kitchen floor, pregnant, crying, and picking up the hamburger helper off of the floor with police officers standing in the kitchen along with Terry's sisters. Then in walked my father who just looked at me like it hurt him to see me like this, saying, "Oh, Melanie." That night, the police had Terry leave so things could calm down. I did not get arrested as I did not burn Terry. My child A'marie went with Terry's sisters for the night. Terry's father was arrested that night at my house when he came to help for a past ticket, warrant, or something. I just don't remember the exact reason.

Terry then moved out. He continued to have a relationship with me, but on his terms—living his life and doing what he wanted when he wanted.

February 4, 2005

Terry picked me up on this cold winter day to take me to the hospital. I was in labor a month early. The doctors give me medication since I was in labor early. On February 5, 2005, at 1:06 p.m., my precious son Ashtyn was born, weighing five pounds, fifteen point eight ounces, and nineteen inches long. When he was born, it wasn't excitement on everyone's faces but concern. Something was wrong. My son was born with a small chin and almost no chin at all. The doctors thought he had Pierre Robin syndrome, and after a while, his chin would drop down, which was what I was told. Terry was around but not as supportive as he was during the birth of our daughter. He would come and go while visiting us in the hospital.

Before our son would be discharged home from the hospital, the doctors wanted to test Ashtyn's oxygen level while sitting in his car seat. Terry bought Ashtyn a car seat and brought it up to the hospital. Ashtyn passed sitting in his car seat and keeping his oxygen level above 90 percent, and on February 7, 2005, we were discharged from the hospital.

At home, there were certain protocols we were to follow with our newborn baby. Ashtyn could only lay on his stomach or side. He was not allowed to lay on his back so his tongue didn't fall back and occlude his airway due to his underdeveloped chin. My son had to be fed every three hours around the clock. I would set an alarm for every three hours just to feed him and document how much he ate. The goal was for Ashtyn to eat at least twenty cc of formula every three hours. Despite his facial deformity, Ashtyn was the cutest baby ever with his chubby cheeks, cute button nose, and deep dark-brown eyes.

Monday, February 14, 2005

At 11:20 a.m., Ashtyn had a doctor's appointment today. He weighed five pounds, seven ounces, and he had thrush. Medicine was prescribed and picked up at the pharmacy.

At 3:30 p.m., while I was attempting to bottle-feed Ashtyn, he stopped breathing. Panic set in! All of my nursing knowledge left me for a moment. I was consumed with fear of the worst. After seconds of shock, I went into saving-my-baby mode and placed my baby's body on my arm, cradling his head in my hand then extending my arm out while facing his head down to the floor.

I then began back blows. Within thirty to forty seconds Ashtyn was breathing. Paramedics were called, and my husband was called. The paramedics did not take Ashtyn to the hospital as Terry and I decided we would drive him to the hospital ourselves.

At 8:30 to 9:00 p.m., Ashtyn was being admitted to the hospital for observation. While in the hospital room, his dad attempted to feed Ashtyn. I was paranoid, telling Terry, "I don't know if you should feed him as that's when he stopped breathing on me." Again, while his dad was feeding Ashtyn, his eyes rolled back into his head and he stopped breathing and became lifeless. The nurse called a code blue and initiated CPR. I felt helpless and scared that my baby was dying. I ran out of the room into the hallway, screaming, "My baby!" while crying. I sat down and rocked back and forth, hands over my mouth, hysterically crying and praying. Someone approached me, and all I could ask was, "Is my baby dead?" I was told after one or two minutes of not breathing, he was now stable and breathing. They placed a nasal tube to keep his airway open, and an IV was placed in his head. I held my son's little hand the whole time.

The doctor discussed that they felt Ashtyn may need a tracheostomy. He needed to be transported to the University of Iowa Children's Hospital. Due to the weather, they were unable to transport him by helicopter, so he would need to be transported by ambulance. That cold snowy night, Ashtyn rode in the ambulance, while his dad and I followed in our vehicle. We arrived at the Iowa City Children's Hospital around midnight. After being directly admitted, I stayed in the hospital room with Ashtyn. We held hands as I held him in my arms, and we slept.

Tuesday, February 15, 2005

My son was only ten days old on this day.

At 2:00 p.m., a nurse attempted to bottle-feed Ashtyn. I told the nurse he was acting the same way when he quit breathing on me when I was feeding him, so she stopped feeding him. Dad and I left for a brief moment to check into the Ronald McDonald

House for a place to stay while in Iowa City. When we returned, we were told the nurse gave Ashtyn a feeding with an nasogastric tube through his nose, and afterward, Ashtyn quit breathing. They had to bag him, and then he started breathing. The doctors believe Ashtyn's tongue was occluding his airway. Ashtyn was then assessed by an ENT (ears, nose, throat specialist) with a scope down his throat. Decisions were made that Ashtyn would have to have a tracheostomy placed so he could breathe.

At 7:30 p.m., the hospital staff took my ten-day-old son for surgery. Placing trust in someone to handle your child's care and life takes a lot of strength while you sit and wait.

At 8:00 p.m., surgery had begun. I leaned on the Lord, praying for over an hour. With my eyes closed, I was having a conversation of a lifetime with God. No one has the control or the power but God. Prayer was my strength and my last resort. My child was in God's hands.

At 10:00 p.m., the surgery is finished. The tracheostomy was placed, and Ashtyn tolerated surgery well. Thank you, God. He was on a ventilator and was very sleepy from anesthesia. I stayed the night with my son, never leaving his side.

Wednesday, February 16, 2005

There were so many tubes coming from every direction on my baby. I was overwhelmed by the sight of my baby lying in the infant hospital bed and appearing lifeless. How could a human so little endure so much?

At 8:00 a.m., Ashtyn opened his eyes briefly—a sign of hope. An x-ray of his spine was done.

CAT scan done. Chest X-ray done. Ultrasound of his kidneys done. He was still on a ventilator as they were slowly weaning my baby off.

At midnight, Ashtyn opened his eyes before I left to go stay at the Ronald McDonald House, attempting to possibly get some sleep. Good night, baby Ashtyn.

Thursday, February 17, 2005

At 12:15 p.m., Ashtyn was taken off of the ventilator. He had an initial ten seconds of apnea, and then he began breathing on his own. Respirations were anywhere from thirty to seventy a minute. Good job, baby!

During our stay at the hospital, we had to learn how to change his tracheostomy and care for our child. We had a suction machine, ambu bag, extra trachs, and lots of supplies, along with a foot pulse oximetry to monitor his oxygen levels. I met with social workers. They set up nursing services to come to my home and help care for Ashtyn daily. They assisted with the process of signing my child up for disability. Ashtyn was diagnosed with Goldenhar syndrome.

Ashtyn had a small mandible and prominent cheeks. His right ear was mildly deformed with a hypoplastic lobe. His right ear was small (three centimeters) compared to his left ear (four centimeters). With Goldenhar syndrome, children can be born with a partially formed ear or a totally absent ear or ears. They may have growths of the eyes and possible spinal deformities. It affects facial structure and possibly other body organs. Usually, this affects only one side of the body but at times both. The cause of Goldenhar syndrome is unknown, but there possibly may be a genetic component.

Before taking our child home, we had to pass twenty-four hours of caring for Ashtyn while being monitored by hospital staff to ensure we could care for our child. We also had to pass changing his tracheostomy along with giving him a bath. Our lives were about to change drastically. Thank God I was a nurse and understood Astyn would require a lot of care.

The sad part is, I began to resent Terry. I blamed him. I felt my baby was under too much stress while I was pregnant, caused by Terry's infidelity that caused a delay in my baby's development, resulting in all of his medical diagnoses now and to come.

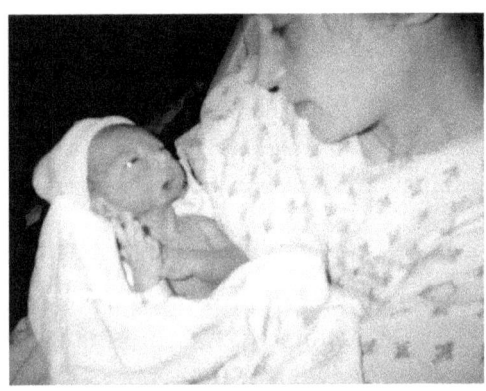

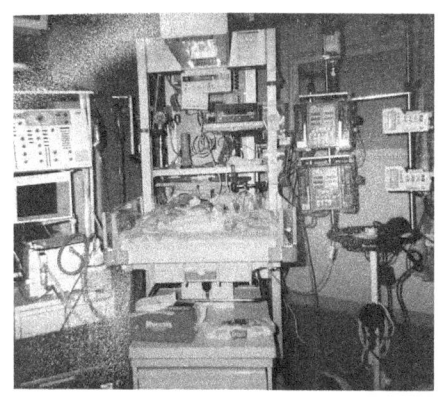

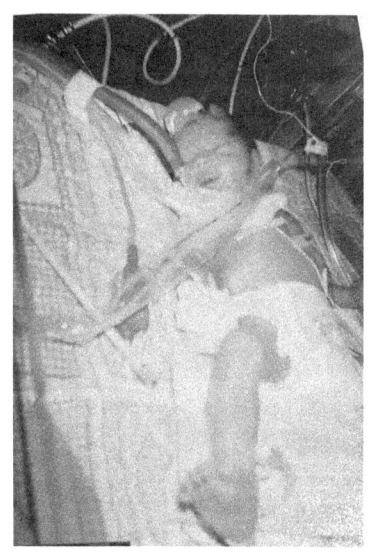

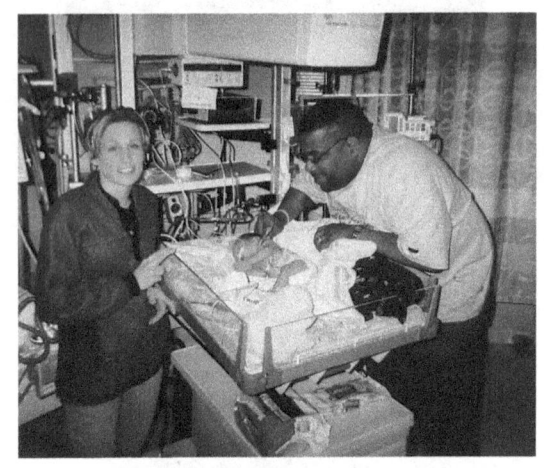

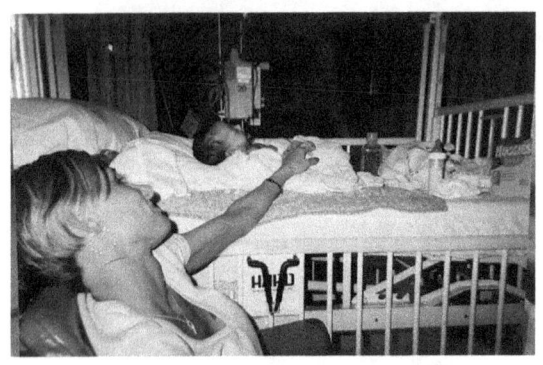

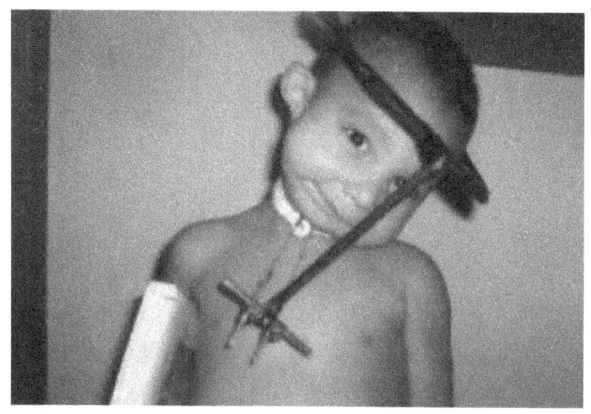

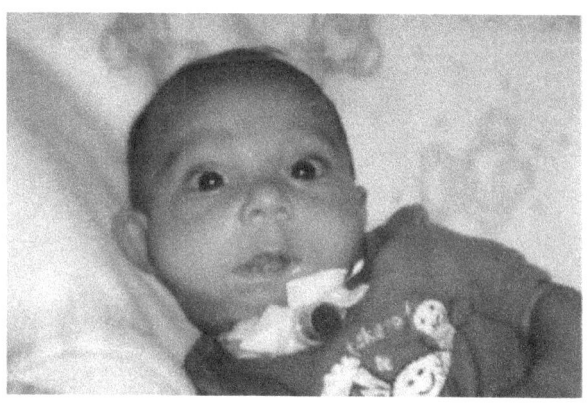

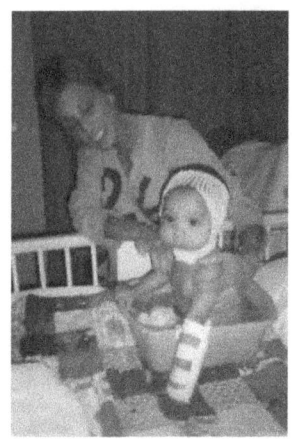

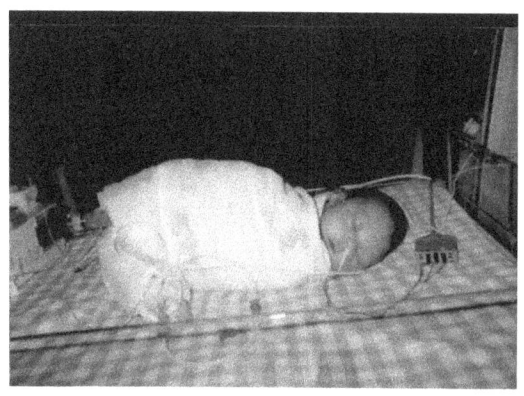

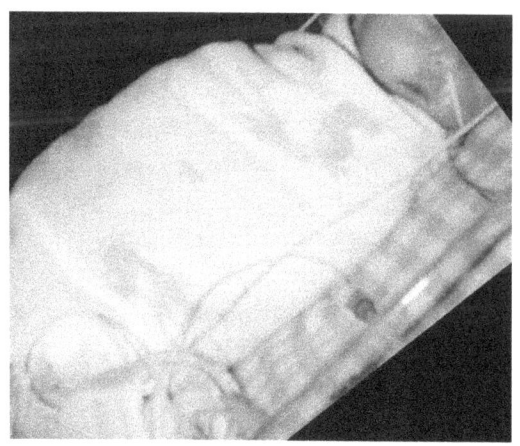

MELANIE CLARK

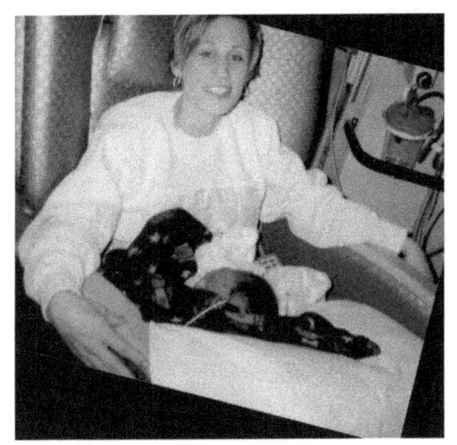

Cancun

Where to begin? Ashtyn was just a month old with a tracheostomy, and nurses were in and out of my home eight hours a day. It was spring break in March 2005, and my husband was "going to Texas for a work trip," or so he told me. I did not believe him. While he was gone, he would call me once or twice a day to check on our family. One day, I decided to call his job to really make sure he was in Texas on a work trip. I called his job and asked them for the hotel information or how I could contact my husband to discuss the medical needs of our baby. They informed me they did not send Terry on a work trip to Texas and were not able to help me. My heart sank to the pit of my stomach even though I wasn't surprised. I was still hurt.

Terry returned to Iowa after being gone a week with a sunburned nose and ears that were peeling from being sunburned. He admitted he wasn't on a work trip to Texas but that he went to visit his friend named Howard in Texas. I still knew something was off and just not right. My intuition was telling me there was more.

Days or a week or more went by, and I received a phone call that shattered my soul and killed me inside. I don't know how to explain the depth of this pain. The mother of an eighteen-year-old girl called me to tell me my thirty-eight-year-old husband took her eighteen-year-old daughter to Cancun over spring break and wined and dined her. I was so numb and distraught that I don't remember the rest of our conversation. Terry denied all of it. Yet I knew it was the truth. The depth of my pain I buried. Eventually Terry moved back home. I felt weak, yet I stayed in our marriage because I needed all the help I could get with our baby with Goldenhar syndrome.

Jamiehr

On September 14, 2007, I started having contractions at around 1:47 a.m. I went to visit my doctor that morning around 11:00 a.m. I was three cm dilated and went home to go on a walk. When I returned home and lay down, Terry informed me I was leaking all over, so we left and headed to the hospital. The nurses and doctors informed me I could stay and walk the halls, go to the mall and walk around, or go home and wait. Terry, my mother, and I decided to go to the mall and walk around, trying to get the contractions started. It didn't take even an hour of walking and I started bleeding, so we returned to the hospital. I was then admitted, awaiting the birth of our son.

Shortly after being admitted, my doctor broke my water; and afterward, I received an epidural. Now the wait began with my husband and mother at my side. While chewing on ice, I remember telling the nurse and my family, "I feel funny. I don't feel right." My blood pressure read 60/26, and the nurse began to hang on the bag of IV fluids as my blood pressure went back up and I began to feel better. My baby continued to do well when this occurred. A little time passed and I told the nurse, "I'm feeling funny again." My blood pressure was very low again, and the nurse hung the bag of fluids as my blood pressure went up and the funny light-headed feeling, like I was going to pass out, went away. Doctors believed that since I was so little and didn't weigh a lot, maybe I received too much of the epidural that was possibly causing my blood pressure to drop. I felt paralyzed in fear at this moment. I had them stop the epidural, and the epidural began to wear off as the pain's intensity increased. I was grateful for this pain. I would rather feel all of the pain and know that my unborn child and I were safe and healthy.

There was lots of pushing. My husband was again at my side, being the best support I could ask for along with my mother and sister-in-law. I was surrounded by love. I remember one intense moment when my son's head was halfway out and the doctor used her fingers to sweep and stretch my vagina as we waited for another contraction to push. I fought through the pressure and pain in that moment, surrendering to God to give us the strength. When another contraction came, it was time to push, with Terry at my side holding my leg and coaching me to breathe and push. Our son was born on September 15, 2007, at 1:47 a.m. We named our son Jamiehr. He was born with a very light complexion, with a head full of a mixture of brown, blonde, and reddish hair. He is the only child of mine that has his mother's green eyes with one bloodshot eye from the pressure in the birth canal and from me pushing. However, we had been blessed with a handsome, healthy baby boy.

Divorce

Staying in a relationship where I was not happy and have exhausted every possibility was not an option anymore for me. Staying could not be healthy for me or my children. They could see and feel everything. I should have left my marriage a long time ago, but after Ashtyn was born with Goldenhar syndrome involving major medical problems and multiple surgeries, I stayed. I tried my best for years to keep my family together. However, so much damage from his infidelity caused me too much pain. I fell out of love with him. I couldn't force myself to just close my eyes, drown out the pain, and have sex with him anymore. It disgusted me. I couldn't just lay here and take it anymore.

I knew that when filing for divorce, I would have to be prepared to deal with Terry fighting dirty because he didn't want to let me go. He didn't want to lose his family. In the past I already filed for divorce once, and Terry fought me every step and caused so much pain and stress for everyone in a matter of days that I had to call off the divorce. I was scared and not prepared.

This time I was as prepared as I could be. I had kept emails at my mother's house of Terry begging me to have sex with him. He also wrote on an envelope one time talking about ending his life. I had secretly been meeting with a lawyer. The day had come that Terry would be served by a sheriff and be asked to leave our home. Well, I don't know how but he found out he was going to be served divorce papers and be removed from the house. Terry went down to the courthouse and went before a judge, claiming I was suicidal and that I abused my children. That he feared for his and the children's lives. That day, I was served first by a sheriff with a no-contact order, and I had to leave my house and not have any contact with my children or Terry for two weeks until I appeared before a judge to prove I was innocent and not guilty of everything I was being accused of by Terry.

Taking my children and home from me with lies killed me inside. I was sick! I wasn't ready for Terry to lie and play this dirty. I had endured so much with this man, and he continued to inflict more pain. Yet this time, I was not giving in. This was cruel to lie about my character as a mother and as a woman. This time, I refused to let him scare me.

During these two weeks, I stayed with my mother. I cried so much, I couldn't cry any more. I lay around numb, feeling sorry for myself and my children. Not being able to see or talk to my children broke me in pieces. I couldn't eat, and I barely could sleep. I was barely functioning. Yet I held on to what strength I had to prove I was not suicidal. I did not abuse my children. Terry was accusing me of all this to be spiteful because I was filing for divorce.

The day of court came, and I was so nervous, feeling sick to my stomach from anxiety. Being on the witness stand under pressure and being questioned is not something I wish on anyone, especially when you are wrongly accused. I am thankful I kept printed emails that Terry sent me in the past and his suicide letter he had written. When Terry took the stand, my lawyer presented Terry with his written suicide letter and asked if he had written this. "Is this your hand-writing?" Terry admitted to writing this letter.

He then looked over at his brother and mouthed, "This bitch is playing dirty," while on the witness stand. He had a look of shock. The emails were also presented to the judge. Also, the DHS worker had spoken to the kids at their school, and the children denied ever being abused by me. The judge then said he needed to review everything, and we would have his decision later that day. It was gut-wrenching for me; still, I had to wait longer for a decision. I was just ready to be home with my children.

Later that day, the judge ruled in my favor. I was not guilty of abusing my children. The no-contact order was dropped. I could go home and see my children. Now Terry was being ordered to leave our home and move out. During this whole year moving forward, Terry refused to come to an agreement and sign the divorce papers until a week before our court date. A week before court, he agreed to meet with my lawyer and I. We came to an agreement, and divorce papers were signed. Prior to our signing divorce papers, I learned that Terry had a son that was born between our son Ashtyn and Jamiehr. Once again before the divorce was final, he found a way to hurt me one more time. He had a child with another woman while we were married and kept it a secret for five years, as this little boy was five years old. Such a double life he lived. I was so grateful to finally be free from him.

On January 6, 2012, our divorce was final. I must say it was bittersweet. Our problem was never that we didn't have love for one another or that we didn't get along. The problem was that Terry was a habitual liar and cheater. When he was finally ready to stop and admitted to regretting everything he had done, it was too late. I had to have more respect for myself for once and end our marriage.

During our divorce, I met someone and started a new relationship. Later in the month of January 2012, I found out I was pregnant with twins. A new chapter of my life was beginning.

Abuse

He was a demon I didn't like to face—a demon I've debated writing about as it gives me PTSD. This man I fell in love with and had twin babies with turned out to be someone I didn't truly know. I lived with him in my own home with my children, and I felt like we were walking on eggshells all the time. I truly feel he has a mental illness, but we will never know. My children and I needed to escape from him. That's when my ex-husband Terry stepped in one day and helped me call the police and get him out of my house. Yet that was just the start of the next few years of hell. During some of this time, I kept a record of what I endured with the twins' father just in case I ever needed proof. Well, that day came.

On Friday, July 21, 2017, at 3:00 p.m., I arrived at the twins' father's one-room apartment to pick up the twins. I stood there, confused and in shock as my daughter Bella's hair looked different. I walked up to her, and she said, "I got my haircut."

I said, "Who cut your hair?"

Her father looked at me and said, "I did!"

Bella's hair was up to the middle of her back, and now it had been cut up to her ears. I stood silently the rest of the time while getting the twins ready to go home.

When we got in the car, Bella said, "Daddy did it in the bathtub. He made two ponytails and cut my hair." Bella was sad and stated, "I did not want my haircut." Bella then said, "He whooped RJ (her twin brother) twice for peeing his pants in his sleep."

RJ then said, "Yeah, and daddy spanked Bella once for peeing her pants in her sleep." This car ride home left me speechless and numb. I was heartbroken for my children who had to endure this treatment from their father.

When we were at home, I asked Bella, "Did you cry after daddy cut your hair?"

Bella whispered in my ear, "I didn't cry. Otherwise, daddy would give me something to cry about."

At around seven o'clock, my daughter and her friend were helping me get the twins ready for bed.

My daughter was giving them a bath when she yelled, "Mom, come here now!" My daughter showed me that RJ had bruises on his lower back, on both buttocks, and on the back of his thighs with perfect circle marks, all like he was beaten with something. Bella had a mark on her neck "from being hit," she said. I was so heartbroken and filled with sadness that this happened to my children. It hurt as a parent that I was unable to protect them.

We got the twins dressed, and I then took them to the police station to file a report against their father for abuse. While at the police station, waiting to speak with a police officer to make a statement, I was holding RJ, and he was making facial expressions of pain. RJ was in pain on his lower back, bottom, and his thighs; and it made it more uncomfortable being held. All I wanted to do was hold my children close to me. After being at the police station for hours, we were then directed that we needed to go to Allen Hospital ER and that a DHS worker would meet us at the hospital. While we were there, the doctors assessed RJ's bruising all over. RJ was in a lot of pain up to his bottom. Pictures were taken. I was instructed that their father was not to see them if he tried. I was informed to call her and the police. The DHS worker stated they would be in contact with the father and she would tell him he was to not see the twins while there was an investigation going on.

In the DHS report, it states, "RJ has over twelve separate distinct marks ranging from his lower back, both buttocks, and then upper thigh areas. They are linear marks leading up to a circular-type bruise with a center area in the middle of the bruised area, which is not bruised, suggesting some type of instrument caused these markings. As this worker was taking photos of RJ's injuries, Bella shared that her daddy hit him with the 'whooping spoon' cause he peed the bed.' RJ also told this worker he was hit by the 'whooping spoon' because he peed the bed. RJ and Bella were consistent in their statements about what happened."

On August 1, 2017, the twins and I had already been through so much in a matter of a few days. We had a DHS worker at our home for a home visit. Today the twins met with Allen Hospital Child Protection Center and were individually interviewed on camera. Later that day, the twins' father showed up at our house to pick up the twins. He was not supposed to and had been informed by authorities. I was not home at this time; however, my older children handled the situation well by showing the twins' father the DHS letter explaining he was not to have contact with the children and that he needed to leave. My children then called me right away. I got home right away and informed the DHS hotline and the police that their father had just been at my home, attempting to pick up the twins when he had been informed there was a no-contact order in place.

On August 3, 2017, DHS note stated:

> There is a warrant out for the arrest of the twins' father on two counts of child endangerment issued today. At 10:30 a.m., father arrived for office visit. DHS worker contacted dispatch to inform father was present at worker's office. DHS worker met with father and advised him any information he provided could be shared with law enforcement. Father advised mom uses the kids to try to get him back together with her. He advised growing up without a two-parent home, as his mother died in childbirth, and wanted his kids to grow up as a family. He then shared when

there were issues in their relationship, he paid for them to go to
counseling. Father advised emotional abuse in the relationship
with Melanie.

He acknowledged physical
issues and being diagnosed with
MS in 2011. He denied issues
with substance abuse, mental
health, or domestic violence.
DHS worker showed father
the pictures of RJ's injuries. He
advised he and Melanie had spoken about RJ peeing the bed.
This conversation was prior to
his last visit with the kids. He also
advised he had taken the kids to
the park earlier that day and RJ
fell on some play equipment balance beam. DHS worker advised
father the marks are specific to a
spoon which the children advised
and such injuries would not have
occurred from a balance beam
fall. He advised he does not have
any such whooping spoon.

Interview was ended as law enforcement arrived and served the warrant. There is a no-contact order issued between the father and twins. He was arrested on two counts of child endangerment. The allegations of Physical Abuse bruise is founded upon the following factors. Physical injury occurred. Both children suffered injuries after their father disciplined/hit them with a spoon. Bella had an injury to her neck, and RJ had multiple specific marks on his lower back, buttocks, and upper thighs indicative of being hit with a wooden spoon as the children reported. The children were very specific every time they were spoken to, sharing the injuries happened after they wet the bed and dad hit them with the spoon. These injuries were not accidental. Both children sustained marks from being hit by their father with a spoon due to wetting the bed/couch where they slept while visiting their father. Father did not accept responsibility and displaced responsibility for this report being made toward the children's mother.

Twins are five years old. They are verbal but unable to avoid situations where they are being hurt especially by a parent. Melanie reacted appropriately after observing the injuries on the children. Melanie did not appear to have an agenda by having the children seen at the police station. Melanie is cooperative with law enforcement and DHS. Father was scheduled to speak with this worker along with law enforcement but canceled that interview at the advice of his attorney. Later he met with this worker at DHS where he was subsequently arrested for child endangerment. Prior to this, the father explained he and Melanie had spoken about RJ peeing the bed and mom not addressing this. He also advised any injuries could have come from playing earlier at the park. Dad feels Melanie uses the twins to try to get back with her. There is currently a No-Contact order between father and children.

This was the beginning of a long, drawn-out case. RJ resorted back to not talking for a while and pointing at things he wanted or needed. He was angry and did not know how to express his emotions properly. We had different agencies in and out of our home, observing the twins and our living structure and my parenting. I complied with all that was asked of me when I did not abuse our children yet understood the importance. Yet their father did not comply with the services he was asked to do. My children and I did therapy together and separately.

On June 8, 2018, "Melanie Clark was awarded sole legal custody and primary physical placement of minor children. The petitioner will have visitation in consultation with the children's therapist. The type of extent, duration, and frequency of the visitation will be determined by the therapist."

To this day, their father has yet to do the things requested by the children's therapist. However, at times he attempts to contact me via Messenger or text, asking me when he can see his children. I refrain from responding as he knows what he has been asked to complete by the children's therapist in order to have visitation with his children.

Family

In this lifetime, my ex-husband Terry touched so many souls. He knew everyone and left an impression no one could forget. He was fun, loud, and the life of the party. He knew how to make you feel seen and heard, feeling important in his presence. Terry was a protector and could always make everything better when he showed up. Terry knew everyone— from a mechanic, car salesman, electrician, attorney, cook, realtor, a tow for your vehicle to a babysitter— and he could always contact someone he knew to help you out.

Yes, he hurt me plenty of times, but there was so much more to him and us that were good. We had a friendship of a lifetime. It was a love for one another that only we understood; it's just that we weren't meant to be married. It just wasn't that "till death do us part" kind of love. Family was everything to Terry, and that is what he stood on and taught me and his children.

Terry taught me it was better to get along with all of his children's mothers for the sake of his children. "Don't stay bitter or resentful over issues. It's the past. Let that shit go!" We wanted the best for our children and to not make them choose which parent they liked or loved the most or what holiday they would spend with which parent. We weren't perfect at this and failed plenty of times, but through the years, we got better and we got along and held it down for all of our children the best we could. Terry showed up for me and the kids. If they had an appointment, he would leave work, as he had that flexibility, and take them. All I had to do was ask, and he made it happen. If they had a sports event or a school function, he was there. If any of us were hungry and called him, he would bring us food or order it and have it delivered to the house. Terry would visit the kids at school, even the twins, and bring them McDonald's for lunch and sit with them. He bought shoes for the kids twice a year. He even bought shoes for the twins; he never made them feel left out. He always said he was their daddy even though he wasn't. Terry would also take all the boys to get haircuts faithfully.

Terry would call all of his children daily. He would call almost every morning, wishing them a good morning and speaking positivity into them to have a good day and to remember, "Be a leader, not a follower." In the summertime, he would come over to my house and mow our lawn weekly. He always had our riding lawn mower taken in for service and maintenance and paid for it. Every winter, when it snowed, he hired someone to plow our driveway at the house.

If there was a tornado watch, he would call and make sure we were in the basement. Terry even went grocery shopping once a month with our children and bought groceries for us. He took care of our home for me and the kids, even though he didn't live here anymore.

We frequently spent holidays together for our children and took family vacations together. Our favorite family get together was boating, fishing, or a great barbecue. He would still come over to my house at times and cook us all supper or grill food. We remained a family even though we were divorced.

Terry visited the house several times a week, and when he did, he always brought me a fountain pop from the convenience store around the corner. He would come over and lay on the couch and let

Bella put makeup on his face along with painting his fingernails with nail polish. We would laugh and laugh at how hilarious he looked, but it was all out of love for the kids. He always wanted me to pick at his ingrown hairs in the back of his head, knowing I loved to pick at things. Terry would always say, "Melanie, where are your tweezers? I need you to get this for me!" He was always hugging me, and I would roll my eyes. But at the same time, I was always grateful for those hugs. He had a deep voice and always dressed nice and smelled good. If I needed him, the majority of the time, he was there for me. I value our friendship and the love we had for our family. Terry had a gift of hospitality. He lived life to the fullest. Most of all, Terry taught all of us the true meaning and importance of family.

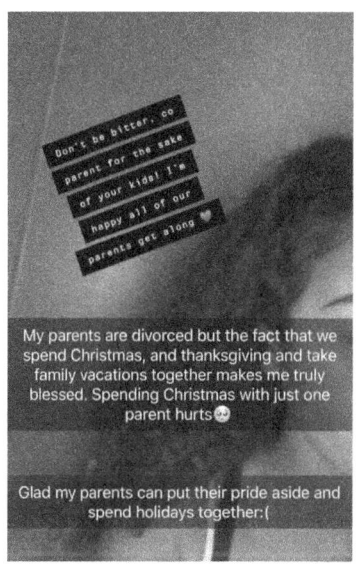

Don't be bitter, co
parent for the sake
of your kids! I'm
happy all of our
parents get along

My parents are divorced but the fact that we
spend Christmas, and thanksgiving and take
family vacations together makes me truly
blessed. Spending Christmas with just one
parent hurts

Glad my parents can put their pride aside and
spend holidays together:(

I've never met anyone that's so happy to mow grass

MELANIE CLARK

COVID-19

As I entered my ex-husband Terry's house to pick up our children, I noticed Terry was lying in bed with a heating pad and covered in blankets as he has the chills in the summertime at that. He said to me, "Feel my forehead. Do you think I have a fever?" I reached over to feel his forehead, and he was on fire.

I immediately backed up and said, "Why did you have me do that? You probably have COVID. Go to the hospital." After the children and I left Terry's house, he drove himself to the hospital. When the children and I were at home, I had them quarantine themselves the best I could as they had even slept next to their father while they were at his house. Later that night, I was notified that Terry had COVID. We had been exposed to COVID.

My daughter called me and asked if I had heard from her father. "I had not." She was concerned as it had been over twenty-four hours and she hadn't heard from him and he wasn't answering his phone. A'marie told me she was going to go to her father's house to check on him. I advised her she needed to be careful because he had COVID. My daughter went to her dad's house, used her key, and went in. She spoke to her father's brother, who was there, and he told her he had been sleeping for days, not showering, not eating much, and he hadn't been taking any of his medications. They were very concerned as he was a diabetic and he had COVID. She got her father to take a shower, take his medicine, and then return to the hospital. Terry was then admitted to Allen Hospital ICU. At this moment, we realized his condition was very serious.

During his stay in the hospital, I was really concerned. He was a family/people person, and he was unable to have contact with any of us physically. I can't imagine the fear he may have had and how depression can set in from not being able to have visitors or see his children. I didn't want him to lose hope. Terry's sister was able to arrange a Zoom call with his social worker for Terry and his children and family. Terry was able to have visual contact with all of us. I am so thankful she did this. We all needed this. I was even able to speak with him for a brief moment. This, I feel, was just what Terry needed to see his family and to give him something to hold onto and fight for. Terry was starting to eventually do better and was transferred out of ICU.

I knew things were still quite serious as power of attorney was discussed. Terry wanted his daughter, A'marie, to make all decisions for him, but she was not eighteen. And the only way that was close to possible was through me. Terry made me his power of attorney over all medical decisions for him. I had to do this for him and our children.

On June 12, 2020, Terry received plasma antibodies and had an allergic reaction. He was then unable to receive the plasma because of the allergic reaction. Later that night, at around 7:00 p.m., Terry's bed alarm sounded, and the nurse reported to me. They thought either he pulled the Vapotherm out or he fell and it came out. The nurse thought he may have been trying to use the bathroom. They found him unresponsive, lying on the floor, and his O2 sats were in the low thirties range. They got his O2 sats up to 60 percent and called a Met Code. A BiPAP was placed on him, and now his O2 sats were 95 percent. He was alert and oriented. The nurse reported he liked the BiPAP better. They gave him something for anxiety. I was told this was the last step before they would use the vent.

I sent out a mass message to family to inform everyone of the situation. I also asked for people to refrain from calling him because he used too much energy trying to talk on the phone with the BiPAP on and it was difficult to understand him. Also, you couldn't understand much of what he was saying on the phone. Terry needed his rest to heal and get better.

On June 13, 2020, at 9:14 p.m., Terry left a voicemail. I couldn't understand a word he was saying. This was very, very, very heartbreaking. Please, Lord, watch over him.

On June 14, 2020, at 6:33 a.m. and 6:41 a.m., he called. Do you know how hard it was not to answer his phone calls? It was the hardest thing I had to do, but I couldn't understand a word he was saying with that BiPAP on. He left voicemails, and you couldn't understand a word he was saying. I felt guilty in the pit of my stomach. I would have given anything to be able to talk to him.

That night, I received a phone call from the hospital that Terry's O2 sats dropped to the eighties. While transporting him back to ICU, Terry had a stroke and coded. I instantly hung up, and my daughter and I rushed down the street from our house to the hospital. A'marie and I arrived at the hospital quickly and entered the ICU where Terry was in a room, with windows all around him, a machine doing CPR compressions, and two nurses gowned, gloved, and masked up, giving him oxygen and injection after injection of epinephrine. I collapsed to the floor, crying, as I watched our daughter standing there just numb, watching CPR being performed on her father. She had a blank painful expression as she just stood there and watched, barely crying. This very moment tore me up and shattered my soul. How could this be happening? I just prayed right there for Terry to fight. I started yelling out loud, "Terry, fight! You got this!" At this moment, he did have a faint pulse, but barely. He was trying to hang on, but slipping away.

We were approached by the doctor as he began talking about, "CPR has already been going on for a while. He has COVID, and he has had a stroke. His chances of survival at this time are slim. Choices will need to be made soon."

A'marie continued to stand there and watched CPR being performed on her father. Then she finally spoke out, "Stop, just stop!" At this time, CPR was stopped. During this moment, Terry's twin brother called and told me to put the phone to Terry's ear. I couldn't as we were not allowed in the room with Terry nor were we able to touch him because he had COVID. Terry's twin brother then told me to give the phone to someone and put it up to his ear! I handed the phone to a nurse, and they put the phone up to Terry's ear as his brother spoke to him. I again fell to the floor and screamed out and cried as Terry held on for a moment, and slowly he kept declining and was pronounced dead at 9:35 p.m.

Terry died from acute respiratory distress syndrome secondary to COVID-19 infection with superimposed pneumonia. A'marie and I were able to gown, mask, and glove up to see Terry and say our goodbyes. We were not allowed to touch him. We couldn't give him one last hug or one last kiss. At this moment, I felt so helpless for my children. Their father was their *everything*! Basically, all we could do was stand there and look at him and pray over him with the pastor. Later that night, when we arrived home to my other children, all of Terry's family followed and visited my home. My daughter Bella screamed and cried as she said, "The wrong father died!"

Terry was cremated. Terry always said, "My home is 157 Sabrina Circle." And now Terry rests in my living room, and I tell everyone, "He is home."

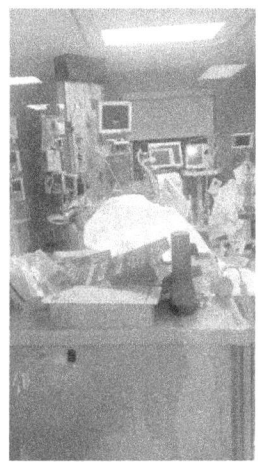

2023 Breast Implants

It had been over twenty years that I have had my breast implants in and I've been cancer free. I currently had the dinosaur edition of breast implants that they don't make anymore. I decided to get new breast implants.

This was a time of change. I was ready for my breast to look and feel more real. I was very hopeful. Due to insurance, surgery would be done in Iowa and not at the Mayo Clinic.

On April 5, 2023, I went to the hospital with my boyfriend, my mother, and my daughter. I had love and support at my side. Surgery went well, and I had the lovely drain tubes in again—this time only one on each side. Pain was mild, not bad at all.

On April 15, 2023, I barely had drainage in my left drain tube, and there was yellow drainage mixed with blood. My left breast was red and hot to touch with swelling. Thanks to my boyfriend, I went to the ER, or I would have waited until the morning. I was being admitted. Now was the hard part. I had an infection in my left breast implant, and I had to have surgery to have the implant removed. I would only have one breast implant, and I would have to wait at least three months. My heart sunk in my chest as I thought, *What the fuck! It's almost summertime, my favorite season to go to the pool daily. Will my boyfriend want me? I just cannot believe this is happening to me. One boob! I really have a problem with this, but I have no choice.*

I was in the hospital for three days, with my boyfriend by my side every step of the way. He even stayed the night with me. For once, I was not alone. Yet I begin to push him away. The summer was hard for me, and I became very depressed. My mental health was fragile, and I began to withdraw and isolate myself. I suffered in silence.

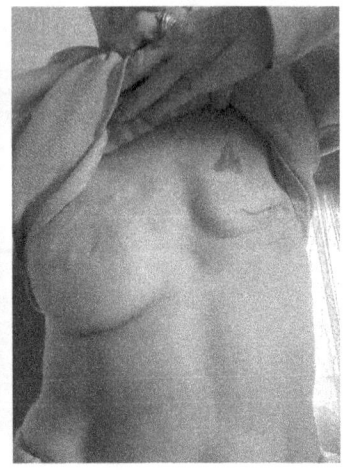

Broken Heart

The love of my life and my soul connection—I broke up with him in August of 2023. Stupid! Depression! I was so ashamed, lost, and hurt. I made a mistake and lost the man I love with every fiber of my being. I was stubborn. I had been heartbroken for months. I was just a hot mess and completely lost. I couldn't stop crying and hurting. I lost all my weight I worked so hard to gain. This loss of my love that I caused had taken my appetite. I was barely functioning. I hadn't had a soul connection like this with a man since Deshawn in high school.

I did something I've never done before: beg. I begged and pleaded for him to take me back, but he had moved on. During the past six months, he contacted me, and we have talked. He came over for Thanksgiving to eat and take a plate home to his mother. A few months later, he contacted me, stating, "I hope you are doing good. I am fucked up, period. I want or need what we had. I want it/need it. My life is fucked up, and I'm losing my fucking mind honestly. I'm functioning but personally miserable. I don't know what I'm trying to say, but fuck I do miss you."

Time went by, and eventually, one night, we met at his house. We hung out and put together a train set. Later that night, we made love, and he would look at me in my eyes. I felt the love and the passion. We started talking again. He even texted me, "Believe it or not, I'm coming back to you." This meant the world to me as I should never have let him go. I missed all of football season and watching football with him, but we watched the Super Bowl at his house together and fell asleep together on the couch. After that, he became distant. He was avoiding me, and he wouldn't respond to text messages at times. And other times, he would avoid me. This was never his normal behavior; he was always very attentive. Come to find out he had not broken it off with the other woman he was seeing. He was having a hard time as her feelings were involved, and he didn't want to hurt her too. He was torn with how to handle the situation.

Then one day, he texted me, "I am not going to manipulate you or anything. I was and am straddling the fence, and that's not fair to you. And I am sorry for that, and I just am trying to get back to a normal I am used to and need. I believe we can or we will have an opportunity to make a way. I am sorry for hurting you, and I know that doesn't make you feel better. But I never wanted to hurt you like this." It hurt so bad. Why did he pull me in and say he was coming back to me when he was still seeing the other woman and lying? The disrespect. I believed he loved me, but this was not love. What a fool I felt like.

Forgiving myself has been a work in progress. He was the one whom my soul loved. Picking up the pieces and getting back to me has been a real struggle. The pain was unbearable at times. I will forever love him, and I have to live with my mistake and heartbreak. I will forever grieve for the life we might have had together.

Return to Mayo Clinic

On November 29, 2023, My daughter and I took the two-hour drive to Mayo Clinic. I was seeing a new surgeon. She had been referred to several times as "the best." This was reassuring. I had new medical insurance now, so I was able to have the procedure done at Mayo Clinic because I refused to have them done again in Waterloo, Iowa. For me, every time has been a terrible experience in Waterloo regarding my breast.

While meeting with the surgeons, I was informed they no longer put breast implants behind the chest wall. It was all about giving the patient a realistic breast. Well, for over twenty years, I had been used to a round, hard breast that didn't move, and I didn't have to wear a bra or own one anymore. They always were sitting pretty. This was the first hurdle. I would have different breasts that I had not been used to.

I was looking forward to having surgery ASAP at the beginning of the new year. I wanted to get back to me. I feel robbed of my womanhood. I wanted to enjoy my life again. Now for the bomb to drop. "The surgeon is booked out for a year, but she is the best." Immediately, tears fall uncontrollably. My daughter was watching her mother at her weakest moment, as she was trying to be hopeful for me. Yet I couldn't stop sobbing. I was informed that in three months, they would contact me, and we would then schedule for a surgery. I could be put on a cancellation list, so I may not have to wait a year. The nurse gave me a website to look at different breasts, so I could get an idea of what I want.

I was hopeful; now I was numb. It was just one big pity party for me. I was heartbroken from losing my boyfriend and now shattered from having to wait for a new breast. The lesson here is, I don't get what I want when I want it. It's a tough pill to swallow.

As we left the office at Mayo Clinic, I stole the box of tissue as I couldn't stop crying. My depression was real; again, I felt so lost and alone.

Breast Prosthesis

My doctor wrote a referral for a breast prosthesis per my request since I would have to go months without one breast. Being out in the community, knowing I had one breast, and feeling like people could take one look at me and know made me feel uncomfortable. I hid out in my house as much as I could. My appointment couldn't come fast enough.

When I met with the specialist to be fitted for a breast prosthesis, we went over insurance. I was informed my insurance through the hospital did not cover a breast prosthesis through them. I was devastated. Every time I think or feel something is finally going to work, there is a roadblock. I started crying in the office. I didn't want to wait any longer. I wanted to feel like a woman to some degree while out in the public. Even if it was just an outside cover-up, no one

would know unless I told them. This whole situation had me flipping emotional. The worker brought
up that they had donated breast prosthesis and bras
from past clients; maybe one would work out for me
until my insurance changed with my new job that
I was about to start. This lady took me to a room
and had me undress from the waist up. She then gave
me a silk robe to provide comfort and privacy while
she went and got the donated breast prosthesis and
bras. She returned and was so kind and gentle with
me and my feelings and needs. We found a breast
prosthesis that was close enough to my other breast
implant. It was just a little smaller. She then fitted
me with two donated bras. While in this room, my
tears began to ease off, and I was able to regain my
composure. I couldn't thank this lady enough for her
generosity and compassion toward me. That day, I
walked out of there wearing a breast prosthesis and
bra. I felt relieved. I could now hide the fact I only
have one breast.

Wearing a bra for the first time in over twenty
years was uncomfortable. I was so used to not wearing a bra. I felt so free not wearing a bra, and now
I felt constricted and trapped in this contraption of
support. I knew with time, I would get so used to a
bra again that I wouldn't even know I was wearing

one, I hoped. More than anything, I was at peace with myself for once, now that I had a breast prosthesis and I could face the hardship of losing my womanhood breast cancer took from me. So yes, they were fake as the real ones tried to kill me a long time ago, but I was still fighting to stay strong with every situation that got thrown at me, trying to knock me down. I may fall at times, but I will always get back up.

Months later, after working at my new job and having new insurance, I requested a new referral from my doctor. I felt that if I had to wait a year or longer for reconstruction and new breast implants, I might as well get fitted for my own breast prosthesis that wasn't donated, along with bras and a swimsuit for the summer. It was time to get back to me and get my shit together. I was tired of the pity party I'd created for myself.

I was fitted for a brand-new breast prosthesis along with four brand-new bras. It was a start in the right direction while I waited patiently for surgery. I was grateful beyond what words can express for my life, for second chances, and for time to make better choices and get this thing called life right, if there is such a thing as getting it right. It was time to live my life to the fullest.

My Father

Growing up as a little girl, I had the best daddy. I adored him. My father was rough and tough on the exterior, and he could scare people with his looks. He had dark long black hair that he would wear in a ponytail with a full beard and a rough masculine voice when he spoke. He wasn't a big man, but his demeanor made you feel uneasy if you didn't know him. I felt proud and protected, as a daughter should. I felt special knowing my dad named me Melanie. My childhood was wonderful with memories I cherish. My daddy worked at the railroad, and I remember when he would come home as a little girl; I wouldn't let him in the house until I knew he brought me home some kind of treat like it was a game. I was always focused on the reward. He made me feel so special, bringing me a roll of paper from the railroad to color on or candy of some kind, but he always remembered to bring me something. My dad liked to listen to Fleetwood Mac, Bob Seger and the Silver Bullet Band, John Cougar Mellencamp, and others while burning candles or making candles and messing with his guns or making bullets. I loved to dance and sing to his music for hours. Making bullets was the best. Daddy would take me out to the shooting range, and I would help him look for brass. I was so good at it. Then after we had enough brass, Daddy would melt it down, and then he had a machine at home that made bullets.

It was so much fun to pull the handle down on the bullet maker. Another fond memory I cherish is when Taco Johns used to have two tacos for ninety-nine cents on Taco Tuesday. He would purchase us some tacos and take me to a lake or pond. We would sit outside, eating our tacos and enjoying nature, and afterward, Daddy would teach me how to skip rocks on the water. Making that ripple effect on the water with a rock gave me so much excitement!

My father did a lot of hunting of squirrels, pheasants, and deer throughout my childhood. As a little girl, I remember my father cleaning these animals after being shot and cutting the meat up to eat. I liked when we did the pheasants as I loved the feathers. I was never too fond of him shooting the deer, as I thought they were beautiful creatures, and I didn't like the thought of killing them. A treasured memory of mine is when they used to sell a cassette tape with a book and you could listen to the story being told as you followed in the book. My daddy used to buy these for me from all the different Disney stories. He would give me his big headphones to plug in to listen to the story; I'm sure it was so he didn't have to hear it, but I felt so special that Daddy would give me his headphones to use. Also, as a little girl on Valentine's Day, my dad would buy me a special big "I love you" chocolate bar.

One of my favorite stories my parents would tell me involved us camping as a family at Yellow River Forest in the woods. My father was drinking peppermint schnapps with ice cubes. My dad gave me an ice cube to suck on out of his drink as it was very hot out. Later that night, I was acting really goofy, as if I were a little tipsy. They realized I had continued to sneak ice cubes out of my dad's glass that night, which caused me to appear drunk. I can only imagine the laughter along with the frantic concern of their little girl appearing drunk.

Summertime was the best as a little girl. My dad's side of the family took a family vacation every year to Crane Lake in Minnesota! We would stay in cabins. I was young and don't remember a lot, but I do remember picking blueberries and making blueberry pancakes, going boating on the lake, swimming in the lake, and getting a helicopter ride over the lake. We would go on hikes, and there were these rocks we stumbled upon that formed like a kid's chair. I loved sitting on it and having pictures to remember. I remember watching bears eat people's garbage out of garbage cans. Most of all, I loved going to the shop that sold Indian moccasins, beaded jewelry, and Indian maracas with beads. They also had this amazing candy I loved. As I reflect on cherished memories, the best part of our vacations was spending time with my great-grandmother, grandmother, aunts, uncles, cousins, and parents.

We lived a block away from Liberty Park, and one year during My Waterloo Days, a hot-air balloon was out flying one night. My father witnessed the hot-air balloon landing at Liberty Park, so he grabbed me and we walked over to see what was going on along with other neighbors in the neighborhood. While at the park, the people that landed the hot-air balloon started giving up-and-down rides to people in the park. My father did not get in the hot-air balloon, but I did. Let me tell you how frightened

I was. The basket to the hot-air balloon was very tall, and I was so small and petite, I couldn't see over the basket. I was standing next to strangers, crammed in a hot-air balloon basket as extremely loud fire blasts started to fill the hot-air balloon, causing it to go up. I cried during this quick ride going up and down as each loud blast of fire startled me. I felt relief after getting out of that hot-air balloon into my daddy's arms. Later in life, I can at least say, "I've been in a hot-air balloon thanks to my daddy!"

Later in my childhood, at some point, my father was injured while working at the railroad. The safety equipment broke, causing my father to hold on for dear life as he hung on and dangled off of the train. This caused my father back injuries that he never truly recovered from. My father sued the railroad, was awarded a settlement, and never worked again.

There was another side of my father as a young girl I witnessed. I witnessed my father abuse my mother. I will never forget the time he was choking my mother by the neck, up against the wall, and her feet weren't touching the ground as her face was beet red. I ran out of the house so fast to the neighbor's house to call the police. Another time, I remember my mother getting her head sliced open and my mother having to go to the hospital to get stitches. I remember a story of scissors in a paper sack and my father threw the sack at her and the scissors sliced the top of her head open. I remember my father following my mother while she was driving and throwing a bowl of refried beans from Taco John's on her window. Also, there was one night my father carved the word *whore* in our front door and would open our house window, cutting the screen with his knife and attempting to get in the house as he yelled, "You don't want me to show your dad something about his innocent daughter!" I also remember staying at an abuse shelter with my mother with other ladies and their children that had been abused by their spouses. I was so young, but this is what remains in my core memories.

My parents divorced when I was in third grade. My father did not take it very well. I didn't take it very well. I remember crying at school about their divorce and having to speak with a counselor as it is hard for any girl to see her daddy move out of the house. Some of those abuse experiences happened after my parents were divorced through the years. My father wouldn't leave my mother alone. He also wouldn't help with his children very often unless my mother was back with him or doing something to benefit him. Around fifth or sixth grade, maybe before that, my parents were back together as it is easier raising children together than apart.

At this time, my dad was home all the time since he didn't work, and my mother worked all the time as a waitress, being the sole provider of the family. And through the years, she went to college too. My relationship with my father became strained, especially once middle school began.

How strict does a father have to be to a young teenage girl that is just trying to do everyday normal teenage activities with her friends? My friends all hung out at the mall on Saturday afternoons and went to the skating rink to roller skate at night. In the summer, they would go to teen dances on Friday nights. Most of my friends had their own telephone in their room and could talk for hours on the phone with their friends. My father would not let me talk on the phone to boys at all, and I could only talk on the phone for five minutes, or sometimes longer, to my girlfriends. When I was on the phone, he would monitor my calls and tell me when it was time to wrap it up and get off the phone. I would clean and clean the house before asking to go skating with my friends, and my friends would be waiting on me for my father's answer, only for my dad to be smiling and laughing in my face while I begged to go skating too then telling me at the last minute, "No," never having a reason why. It was a real big letdown.

It always felt like a cruel game that my father found sick pleasure in that I had no choice but to play. I could barely go to the mall on Saturdays to just hang out with my friends. You see, I liked or was attracted to boys that were a different color than me, and my dad was trying to keep me away from black boys the best way he could. Preventing me from doing normal teenage activities and hangouts with my friends led me in another direction. I started rebelling, having behaviors at home with my father like having a smart mouth and learning to defend myself and others. I began sneaking out of my window at night, which led me to having sex at fourteen years of age. All of what my father was trying to prevent actually pushed me in that direction. All I wanted to be was a normal teenage girl, and instead I had to sneak around, which led to poor decisions on my behalf.

Through the years I was called a nigger lover and a nigger bitch by my own father. What unfair treatment to reflect such hate and anger on your own child. I refused to be silenced and fought back for what I believed in. I refused to let his malicious judgment and prejudice modify how I saw other humans in the world. I believe in loving everyone and not judging others by the color of their skin.

In my first year of high school, in the middle of the semester, my father bought our family a house in Cedar Falls. My father was attempting to get me away from the "black boys." I was so angry, as ninth-grade students in the Cedar Falls School district were still in middle school. I had to go from high school back to middle school. I refused to go to school for days as I needed time to accept and deal with the change. I couldn't change getting the courage to experience the unfamiliar, to go back to middle school and begin to make new friends.

Freedom became easier for me when I was able to have a job and get my own car. I was *never* home. There were some nights I never even went home and would stay at my boyfriend's or a friend's house. Do you know what it is like to have a home and it doesn't feel like home? I was always walking around on eggshells around my father. My mother was barely around as she worked all the time or went to school, and she was the only person who understood me and did her best to fight for me. I know I wasn't the most pleasant to live with at this age as I had a smart mouth and thought I knew it all, but I was just crying out for understanding, a love without judgment, acceptance, some kindness, a little patience, and my father's love.

I wanted to get pregnant so I could get away. I saw getting pregnant as my only escape from my father and his cruel views and punishment toward me. The verbal and mental abuse I endured for loving a person of a different color broke me. I hated my father for a very long time.

I thought having a baby was the only way out! When it finally happened at the age of seventeen, I did move out with Deshawn into our own apartment with friends. I loved being on my own in an environment where I could be myself and be happy. Deshawn was more than good to me, and I was blessed that we shared a love and connection with one another and were beginning our life together as a family.

When Deshawn was killed in 1995 and I was six months pregnant, my father was the one who told my mother, "Get her home. Haven't you ever heard of Romeo and Juliet?" I moved back home, and my father started to change and our relationship began very slowly to be restored.

He was the best grandfather ever to his grandson that was half white and half black; it touched my soul. It began to heal the parts of me and how I viewed my father by the way he loved my son.

Deshawn was always at my father's side, his buddy! My father loved Deshawn like his own, and my father became the closest thing to a father my son would know. I always say Deshawn got the best years of my dad. The things he couldn't do with me or for me, he did with and for my child. Deshawn experienced so many fun adventures with my father and knew parts of my dad I never knew. That part right there touched my heart and meant everything to me. That was a father's love for his daughter and grandson.

Later on in my twenties, my father and mother finally parted ways. My father again was hurt, but I feel it was the best thing for him. He changed. He was more kind, more loving, and did more for himself. He was very bitter about the situation and would not attend anything that my mother would be at. This caused his children to pick and choose which parent they wanted at certain events or occasions in their lives. I accepted his choice, but I refused to participate and choose which parent to have at certain functions or special moments in our lives. My father missed out on a lot in my life as far as being there or around when his daughter went through breast cancer. He missed my wedding and the births of my children, along with many other occasions all because of his stipulation to not be anywhere around my mother. I feel he only did that as he hurt so badly because he really loved her and wanted a life and his family back, which destroyed him to his core.

When Terry and I started house hunting, my father was with us when we found our home. That day, my father lent us the money to put down as an offer on our forever home. He was there for my husband and I that day, and I am forever grateful.

When my father was able to apply for railroad retirement, he got denied. I assisted him in reapplying and since I am a nurse, I was able to help him fill out the form more correctly and he was approved. My father personally delivered to my front door a thank-you card with a one-hundred-dollar bill for helping him get approved. What meant the most was the handwritten note attached to the card that read, "I know who I can depend on. You made me very proud of you." These are words I've longed to hear for years. It's very touching, so touching that I have them tattooed on my forearm in his handwriting.

My father became ill in 2015 and was at the University of Iowa Hospital. I received the worst call I was never ready for on July 16, 2015; a doctor called me and informed me they were doing CPR currently as we spoke on my father. I screamed and freaked out and told them I was leaving now and would be right there. I stormed out of the house, trying to call my brother, but no one could reach him. I was able to contact his wife and inform her of the situation. Now, Iowa City Hospital is about an hour away from my house, and while driving there, the doctor called me again and said, "We have been doing CPR for a while, and at this point, he is brain dead."

I interrupted her and told her to "stop the CPR. This is not what my dad wants. He never wanted to be a full code and have CPR be performed on him." When I arrived at the hospital, my father was dead and still had the mouth tube in place. I begged for them to take it out. After they took it out, I climbed into the small gurney bed with him and hugged him so close, burying my face in his chest as I cried and cried until my brother and his wife arrived.

My father, Larry P. "Pat" Clark, sixty-two, of Cedar Falls, died at the University of Iowa Hospitals and Clinics, on Thursday, July 16, 2015, after a brief illness. Pat was born on March 17, 1953, in Waterloo, the son of Marvin and Loretta Eldridge Clark. He graduated from West High School with the class of 1972. He married Michelle Remetch in Waterloo in 1976, and they were later divorced. Pat worked as a brakeman for the Illinois Central Railroad for many years. Pat was a simple and easygoing man who had a gruff exterior but a heart of gold and also a bit of a mischievous side that he would show to his family and close friends. He had a love of nature and enjoyed going for walks and hunting. Pat was a true history buff and could even point out errors in history books. Twinkies would always accompany his milkshakes, and his root beer had to be A&W. He didn't need a lot of friends, but he found it more important to be closer to the few friends he had. Pat loved spending time with his grandchildren and would always have Hershey Kisses around for them.

The nicest and most meaningful thing that touched my heart was, when asked his religion, my aunt responded, "Nature."

The most hurtful gesture my family and I endured during the passing of my father was the fact the twins were unable to attend my father's funeral. The day of the funeral did not land on my scheduled day to have the twins, so their father would not work something out with me so they could attend their grandfather's funeral. Granted, the twins were little, and it did not affect them at the time. Knowing about it now the older they have gotten, they feel sorrow and some type of emptiness from knowing they were not allowed to be there. Any time the twins' father could make life hard for me, he did. His behavior was familiar as I remember my own father in my childhood acting the same way to my mother. The anxiety and sorrow I felt from this form of abuse ate at my soul. Yet I had to be as strong as always and just accept the hand I've been dealt.

Since my father passed away, I find feathers all the time. On my way to an interview for a new job, there was a feather in my path. I picked it up and said, "Thank you, Daddy." When having a bad day in the middle of winter, I'll find a feather in my car. There is a saying that goes, "When feathers appear, angels are near." I believe my father leaves me feathers, and each time I pick them up and save them, I feel—in fact, I know—it is my father's way of communicating with me. I have a collection of feathers now, all from my daddy, I believe.

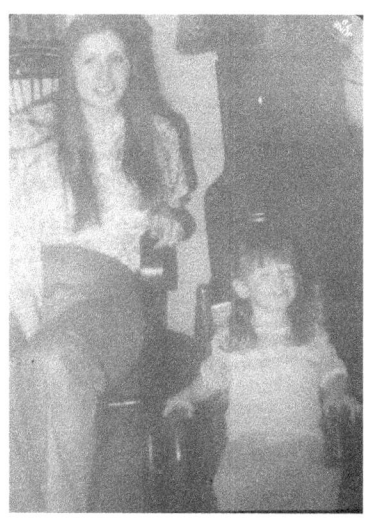

Forgiveness

"Forgiveness is just another name for freedom" (Byron Katie).

When you choose to forgive, you experience true freedom. I have learned and believe that to be very true. Forgiveness is a choice one has to make and pursue. It releases feelings of resentment, anger, and ill feelings toward another, and it provides rest for your soul. Forgiveness is never easy; it takes time, and it doesn't happen all at once. It doesn't mean you forget whatever has happened; forgiveness just allows you to move forward in life. Forgiveness is not for the person who hurt you; it is actually for you as it offers you your own mental healing of not letting that person have power and control over you. You waste time and energy being angry and resentful toward another person. I refuse to let my anger steal my energy and joy for very long. I don't want to be a bitter person hung up on past wrongs that one has made, as we are all human and make mistakes. Forgiveness can lead to feelings of empathy, compassion, and understanding for the ones who have hurt you, which leads to healing.

Through the years, I have had to learn to forgive my father, Deshawn, David, Terry, and the twins' father. Most of all, I've forgiven myself for bad decisions and for the times I lacked understanding. Definitely for choices I made that either hurt me along with being young, naive, and at times, reckless. These are all just vital lessons that life hands us, causing us to grow as an individual. Holding onto pain is a terrible way to live.

"Love is an act of endless forgiveness. Forgiveness is me giving up my right to hurt you for hurting me. Forgiveness is the final act of love" (Reinhold Niebuhr).

Searching

All these years, I've been searching for the answer! Tell me what to do, how to live, and how to make it better. What's my purpose? What's the meaning of life? What about love and relationships? Right and wrong? How do I be a better parent? How do I deal with trauma? What is grief? How do I deal with death? What did I do wrong? Am I a bad person? How do I be positive? How do I manifest? How do I pray? What about God? How do I be a better human? How do I be successful? How do I just make it in life?

I'm always buying books, searching for an answer. However, I don't find the answer, just advice. Everyone has an answer/opinion, but there is never one true, definite correct answer. Life is joy, pain, happiness, a struggle, a mountain to climb, a moment to treasure, a blessing, and so much more. You learn and figure it out as you go as life has teachable moments. Life is not fair. Life is what you make it. Life is a choice. We all have choices to make, and we learn from those choices. There is no way to avoid pain and struggle in our lives; otherwise, how would we know how to value and cherish all the love, happiness, and blessings along life's journey?

Why?

Why me? Why not me? Everything that has happened to me so far in my life has just been a reminder that God is in charge, and I need to trust him with all my heart and learn to have patience.

Through the years, I have often questioned God. Am I being punished for something I did or didn't do? Why would God make me suffer so much in my life? Why me? The real question is, Why not me? I am no better than any other human on this earth, and I know for sure I am not more righteous than God. I am a sinner. I have free will. I can be led by temptation at times.

I heard somewhere that suffering is actually a blessing. Suffering has a purpose in our lives, and sometimes God shows us his power through our pain, suffering, and struggles. In life sometimes, we choose to look away and drift from God and his word. I believe it's called backsliding, believing we can live life without him. Well, God has a way of bringing us all back to him.

Love Yourself

When I look back on my life, I see a plethora of mistakes, bad choices, heartache, and a lot of pain. I am not perfect; I never will be. I believe in not judging others for their past mistakes or the color of their skin. I believe people learn and grow. That's life!

When I look at myself in the mirror now, I don't see those mistakes, I see strength and lessons learned that have made me the woman I am today. Most of all, I have joy and pride in myself. All I've endured has shaped me into a grateful human with positive energy and a beautiful soul. I am a rare gem.

Don't give up! Become so confident in who you are, becoming one with the choices you've made throughout life. No one's opinion, behavior, or rejection should ever knock you off your feet, and if it does, get back up. Always give yourself the time you need and require. Most importantly, *go love yourself!*

Now I would like to leave you with my keepsakes. These are poems, quotes, and important information that mean something to me that I want to share with you. In times of need and reassurance, some of these words gave me something to believe in and make it through.

Prayer for Serenity

God, grant me the serenity to
    accept the things I cannot
    change
The courage to change the things
    I can
And the wisdom to know the
    difference
Living one day at a time
Enjoying one moment at a time
Accepting hardship as a pathway
    to peace
Taking, as Jesus did
This sinful world as it is
Not as I would have it
Trusting that you will make all
    things right
If I surrender to your will

So that I may be reasonably
        happy in this life
And supremely happy with
        you forever in the next.
        (Reinhold Niebuhr)

This is from *Untamed* by Glennon Doyle, and here's an excerpt from her book:

> We hurt people, and we are hurt by people. We feel left out, envious, not good enough, sick and tired. We have unrealized dreams and deep regrets. We are certain that we were meant for more and that we don't even deserve what we have. We feel ecstatic and then numb. We wish our parents had done better by us: We wish we could do better by our children. We betray and we are betrayed. We lie and we are lied to. We say goodbye to animals, to places, to people we cannot live without. We are so afraid of dying. Also: of living. We have fallen in love

and out of love, and people have fallen in and out of love with us. We wonder if what happened to us that night will mean we can never be touched again without fear. We live with rage bubbling. We are sweaty, bloated, gassy, oily. We love our children, we do not want children. We are at war with our bodies, our minds, our souls. We are at war with one another. We wish we'd said all those things while they were still here. They're still here, and we're still not saying those things. We know we won't. We don't understand ourselves. We don't understand why we hurt those we love. We want to be forgiven. We cannot forgive. We don't understand God. We believe, we absolutely do not believe. We are lonely. We want to be left alone. We want to belong. We want to be loved. We want to be loved. We want to be loved.

If this is our shared human experience, where did we get the idea that there is some other, better, more perfect, unbroken way to be human? Where is the human being who is functioning "correctly," against whom we are all judging our performances? Who is she? Where is she? What is her life if it is not these things?

If you are uncomfortable—in deep pain, angry, yearning, confused—you don't have a problem, you have a life. Being human is not hard because you're doing it wrong, it's hard because you're doing it right. You will never change the fact that being human is hard, so you must change your idea that it was ever supposed to be easy.

*****

To Those I Love...and Those Who Love Me...

When I am gone, release me, let
     me go—
I have so many things to see and
     do.
You mustn't tie yourself to me
     with tears,
Be happy that we had so many
     years.

I gave you my love. You can only
     guess
How much you gave to me in
     happiness.
I thank you for the love you each
     have shown,
But now it's time I traveled on
     alone.

So grieve a while for me if grieve
     you must
Then let your grief be comforted
     by trust.
It's only for a while that we must
     part
So bless the memories within
     your heart.

I won't be far away, for life goes
    on
So if you need me, call and I will
    come.
Though you can't see or touch
    me, I'll be near.
And if you listen with your heart,
    you'll hear
All my love around you soft and
    clear.

And then, when you must come
    this way alone,
I'll greet you with a smile
    and "Welcome Home."
(Unknown)

*****

Life is an opportunity, bene-
    fit from it. Life is beauty,
    admire it.
Life is a dream, realize it.
Life is a challenge, meet it.
Life is a duty, complete it.
Life is a game, play it.

198

Life is a promise, fulfill it.
Life is a song, sing it.
Life is a struggle, accept it.
Life is a tragedy, confront it.
Life is an adventure, dare it.
Life is luck, make it.
Life is too precious, do not destroy it.
Life is life, fight for it. (Mother Teresa)

Sometimes the people who hurt us the most are people who were hurt more than us. (Philppos)

I have found the one whom my soul loves. (Song of Solomon 3:4)

I believe that two people are connected at the heart, and it doesn't matter what you do, or who you are, or where you live. There are no boundaries or bar-

riers if two people are destined to
be together. (Julia Roberts)

You are my blue crayon.
The one I never have enough of.
The one I use to color my sky. (A.
R. Asher)

He's rough and tough on
the exterior but inside a gem-
stone of the rarest find, he's bad
boy vibes but loves me good, and
that's a man of the best kind. (D.
L. Smith)

Do you want me to tell you
something really subversive? Love
is everything it's cracked up to be.
That's why people are so cynical
about it. It really is worth fighting for, being brave for, risking
everything for. And the trouble
is if you don't risk anything, you
risk even more. (Erica Jong)

Learn to let go. That is the key to happiness. (Buddha)

Life is a balance of holding on and letting go. (Rumi)

Never let a problem to be solved become more important than the person to be loved. (Barbara Johnson)

We are all of us stars and we deserve to twinkle. (Marilyn Monroe)

Falling in love with someone isn't always going to be easy… Anger…Fears…Laughter… It's when you want to be together despite it all. That's when you truly love another. I'm sure of it. (Michael Jackson)

If you judge people, you have no time to love them. (Mother Teresa)

MELANIE CLARK

What can you do to promote world peace? Go home and love your family. (Mother Teresa)

I love you not only for what you are, but for what I am when I am with you. (Roy Croft)

I gather up each sound you left behind and stretch them on our bed. Each night I breathe you and become high. (Sonia Sanchez)

Into the forest I go to lose my mind and find my soul. (John Muir)

This is a quote about the death of a child/stillborn:

An angel opened the book of life and wrote down my baby's birth. Then she whispered and closed the book, "Too beautiful for earth." (Author Unknown)

Sit with it. Instead of drinking it away, smoking it away, sleeping it away, eating it away, fucking it away, or running from it. Sit with it. Healing happens by feeling. (Author Unknown)

Show me your Soul
Show me
The most damaged
Parts of your soul
And I will show you
How it still shines like gold.
(Nikita Gill)

Love is patient, love is kind, it does not envy, it does not boast, it is not proud. It does not dishonor others. It is not self-seeking. It is not easily angered. It keeps no wrongs. Love does not delight in evil but rejoices in the truth. It always protects, always trusts, always hopes, and always preserves. Love never fails... (1 Corinthians 13:4–7)

The strength of my soul was born on the backs of moments that brought me to my knees. (S. L. Heaton)

Today be thankful and think how rich you are. Your family is priceless. Your health is wealth. Your time is gold. (Zig Ziglar)

You are always responsible for how you act, no matter how you feel. (Robert Tew)

See there's this place in me where your fingerprints still rest, your kisses still linger, and your whispers softly echo. It's the place where a part of you will forever be a part of me. (Author Unknown)

No one changes unless they want to. Not if you beg them. Not if you shame them. Not if you use reason, emotion, or tough love. There's only one thing that makes someone change: Their own realization that they need to do it. And there's only one time it will happen: when they decide they're ready. (Lori Deschene)

The man who is truly sorry, will change his behavior. The man who misses you, will make an effort and always show up. The man who truly loves you, won't make you feel like shit. (R. H. Sin)

You can't just give up on someone because the situation is not ideal. Great relationships aren't great because they have problems. They're great because both people care enough about the other person to find a way to make it work. (Author Unknown)

Do you think you have a choice in loving someone? The answer will always be…no. Your soul picks who you love and your heart seals the deal. How little a choice we have over such things when your heart knows what it wants and your soul knows when it is real. (Author Unknown)

> Go and love someone
> Exactly as they are.
> And then watch how quickly
> They transform into the greatest, truest version of themselves.
> When one feels seen and appreciated in their own essence,
> One is instantly EMPOW-ERED. (wes angclzzi/@ projecthappiness.org)

> God could not be every-where, and so he made mothers. (Jewish Proverb)

> The only way you can live forever is to love somebody—

then you really leave a gift behind. (Bernie Siegel, MD)

The most difficult year of marriage is the one you're in. (Franklin P. Jones)

Blessed is the influence of one true loving human soul on another. (George Eliot)

Wherever you are, I am there also. (Beethoven)

Your heart is not living until it has experienced pain... the pain of love breaks open the heart, even if it is as hard as a rock. (Hazrat Inayat Khan)

God is in the details. (Ludwig Mies van der Rohe)

One word frees us of all the weight and pain of life. The word is "love." (Sophocles)

Two are better than one, because together they can work more effectively. If one of them falls down, the other can help him up, but if someone is alone and falls, it's just too bad, because there is no one to help him. (Ecclesiastes 4:9, 10)

Memory is the gift from God which death cannot destroy. (Kahlil Gibran)

The one thing we can never get enough of is love and the one thing we never give enough of is love. (Henry Miller)

You don't get to choose how you're going to die, or when you can only decide how you're going to live, Now. (Joan Baez)

When you look for the good in others, you discover the best in yourself. (Martha Walsh)

If love does not know how to give and take without restrictions, it is not love, but a transaction. (Emma Goldman)

Watch. Wait. Time will unfold and fulfill its purpose. (Marrianne Williamson)

As every thread of gold is valuable, so is every moment of time. (J. Mason)

Do not complain about growing older—many are denied the privilege. (Robert Russell)

If we really want to love, we must learn to forgive. (Mother Teresa)

…love knows not its own depth until the hour of separation. (Kahlil Gibran)

Do not pray for easy lives.
Pray to be stronger. (John F.
Kennedy)

The best and most beautiful
things in life cannot be seen or
even touched… they must be felt
with the heart. (Helen Keller)

A poet of long ago put the
difference between optimism
and pessimism this way: "Two
men looked out from the prison
bars—one saw mud, the other
saw stars."

Grief is the final act of love.
My heart hears you. I feel you
everywhere. I'm grateful that I
had you. I love you beyond this
earth, and until we meet again,
the marathon continues. (Lauren
London)

Trying to change someone is
a waste of time. The very thought

of changing someone is saying that they are not good enough as they are, and it is soaked with judgment and disapproval. That is not a thought of appreciation, or love, and those thoughts will only bring separation between you and that person. You must look for good in people to have more appear. As you look only for the good things in a person, you will be amazed at what your new focus reveals. (*The Secret Daily Teachings* by Rhonda Byrne, Day 305)

I don't care much for things
That I can't take
With me after I die.
Give me love.
Moments. Purpose.
Things that'll settle in the soul. (A. R. Lucas)

When one door is closed,
don't you know that many more
are open. (Bob Marley)

You may not control all the
events that happen to you, but
you can decide not to be reduced
by them. (Maya Angelou)

At the start of each day,
There is a moment that I
realize That there is a part of me
missing.
Sometimes it's manageable
and Sometimes it's not.
I've been asked many times
To describe what it is that I
feel and it's like
Never being able to find
home again.
Yet I yearn just to be home
One more time This is grief and
loss. (Author Unknown)

Write it down on real paper with a real pencil. And watch shit get real. (Erykah Badu)

One thing I've learned… life is a paradox. In order to love you must break open, in order to have peace you must face chaos. Never regret any experience in your life, because it is always meant to bring you balance. The light always follows. (Author Unknown)

It's easy to judge.

It's more difficult to understand.

Understanding requires compassion,

Patience, and a willingness to believe

That good hearts sometimes choose poor methods.

Through judging, we separate.

Through understanding, we grow. (Doe Zantamata)

The right people for your soul,
　　Hear you differently,
　　Show up differently,
　　Support you differently,
　　And nourish you differently,
　　That's how you will know.
(Author Unknown)

You have escaped the cage. Your wings are stretched out. Now fly. (Rumi)

Embrace uncertainty. Some of the most beautiful chapters in our lives won't have a title until much later. (Bob Goff)

　　Keep going
　　No matter how stuck you feel
　　No matter how bad things are right now

No matter how many days you've spent crying
No matter how hopeless and depressed you feel
No matter how many days
You've spent wishing things were different
I promise you won't feel this way forever
Keep   going.
(*TheMindsJournal*)

Grief is love's souvenir. It's our proof that we once loved. Grief is the receipt we wave in the air that says to the world: Look! Love was once mine. I loved well. Here is my proof that I paid the price. (Glennon Doyle Melton)

Be your own biggest fan, your own biggest believer, and put it on your back and carry the weight. (Nipsey Hussle)

A strong woman loves, forgives, walks away, lets go, tries again, and perseveres...no matter what life throws at her. (Rachel's Heart)

I always find beauty in things that are odd and imperfect—they are much more interesting. (Marc Jacobs)

They both suffer in silence. It was real, it was true, but some things can't be fixed, and that is a damn shame for those loves that were so powerful, those souls that were so connected. There will never be another love quite the same, or even half as intense for either of them. So they continue living, tortured, without each other. (Melody Lee)

When you understand that nothing and no one belongs

to you, your true peace begins. (Author Unknown)

You really don't know pain until you sat somewhere and begged God to heal your heart. (Thinkingminds)

You change for two reasons: either you learn enough that you want to, or you've been hurt enough that you have to. (Kate Mcgahan)

Suggested Books to Read:

- The Bible
- *Fervent* by Priscilla Sirer
- *Imperfect Endings* by Zoe FitzGerald Carter
- *The Alchemist* by Paulo Coelho
- *The Color of Water* by James McBride
- *Gift of Life* by Henri Landwirth
- *Greenlights* by Mathew McConaughey
- *Think and Grow Rich* by Napoleon Hill
- *The Wednesday Letters* by Jason F. Wright
- *The Shack* by William Paul Young
- *Untamed* by Glennon Doyle
- *Finding Me* by Viola Davis
- *The Four Agreements* by Don Miguel Ruiz
- *The Secret* by Rhonday Byrne
- *Change Your Paradigm, Change Your Life* by Bob Proctor
- *The Glass Castle* by Jeannette Walls
- *The Battle Plan for Prayer* by Stephen and Alex Kendrick
- *Fresh Start* by Joel Olsteen
- *Lost and Found* by Sarah Jakes

THE CROSSES I'VE CARRIED

About the Author

Melanie Clark was born and raised in Waterloo, Iowa. She is blessed with six children and one granddaughter. She has worked in healthcare for over twenty years and currently works as an MDS Coordinator. Melanie is a breast cancer survivor, spends her free time with her family, and most of all, loves to travel.